THE HISTORY OF WITLEY, MILFORD AND SURROUNDING AREA

From prehistoric times to 2000

A short history of the development of the landscape and people within the Parish of Witley, including the surrounding villages and hamlets

Dr. Elizabeth Forster BSc.

On behalf of Witley Parish Council, as part of the celebration of the new millennium.
October, 1999

Published by Witley Parish Council.
November 1999.

ISBN © 0 9537619 0 8

Printed by Blackdown Press Limited
Fernhurst, Haslemere, Surrey GU27 3EE

*Front Cover. View of Witley Church from Church Lane with White Hart in the distance.
From a watercolour by H. Sutton Palmer. Reproduced courtesy of A&C Black (Publishers) Ltd.*

The author gratefully acknowledges copyright permission from the following.
Surrey Archaelogical Society for illustrations on page 7;
Haslemere Educational Museum for illustrations on pages 4, 6, 8, 42, 54, 61, 62, 76;
Harry Margary Maps, Lympne Castle, Kent. GT21 4LQ for illustrations on pages 38, 48, 52;
Godalming Museum for illustrations on pages 34 and 55;
A&C Black (Publishers) Ltd. for the front cover illustration;
Phillimore & Co. Ltd, Shopwyke Manor Barn, Chichester, W.Sussex, page 14;
Surrey County Archaeological Unit, page 22;
Surrey History Service, pages 58, 72 and 73;
Guildford Museum, pages 2 and 4.

Fronticepiece: View of the Greensand Escarpment from the old Witley Deer Park.

Acknowledgments

Even as long ago as the Domesday survey in 1086, the settlement and land use patterns of Witley and the surrounding area, were well established. Records of local events can be found in the Court Rolls, the Woods Collection and the Loseley manuscripts. However, to interpret the early days, before the advent of written records, we must seek our evidence from the environment, in the form of pollen analysis, understanding the local geology and interpreting archaeological finds. We are fortunate that members of the Surrey County Archaeological Unit and the Surrey Archaeological Society have done a tremendous amount of work in the area from which it is possible to trace an almost complete record of habitation and settlement development from Palaeolithic times. The detailed results of their work and that of other local historians are recommended for further reading.

The author is grateful to Richard Broad, past historian at King Edward's School Witley for permission to use material as background to the chapter on social changes in the area from the 18th century. Information on the 19th century was kindly provided by Bertie Mawer, Marilyn Wilkes and Hugh Turrall-Clarke. I am extremely grateful to Annabel Watts for providing advice and information on the artists of Witley. I am indebted to Rob Poulton, Head of the Surrey County Archaeological Unit, and to Alan Crocker, President of the Surrey Industrial Archaeology Society, for checking and commenting on the chapters covering the early history and to Bertie Mawer and Marilyn Wilkes for comenting on Chapter 4.

The author thanks Greta Turner and staff at the Haslemere Educational Museum for their interest and cooperation in helping this document to materialise.

THE HISTORY OF WITLEY, MILFORD AND SURROUNDING AREA

From prehistoric times to 2000

CONTENTS

THE HISTORY OF WITLEY, MILFORD AND SURROUNDING AREA

From prehistoric times to 2000

Introduction

The civil parish of Witley lies in the south west of the county of Surrey, covering an area of 11.2 square miles, nearly 7,000 acres, and in the Surrey Hills designated as an Area of Outstanding Natural Beauty (AONB). The River Wey forms the northern boundary in Peper Harow Park and from here the parish extends 9 km to the south, to Grayswood. The ecclesiastical parish of Thursley, which now forms the western margin, was until 1838, part of the ancient Royal Manor of Witley, and the Saxon church at Thursley was a chapel within Witley Parish. The area to the north of Thursley has played an interesting role in our landscape development since the end of the Ice Ages, through the iron and silk manufacture of the 17th and 18th centuries. Now the area is a nature reserve whose particularly rare flora and fauna are of international significance.

To the east of Witley, the civil parish boundary with Godalming now lies at Enton, but until 1905, Enton was within a thin, southerly extension of the Godalming Parish and in ancient times formed part of the Manor of Godalming. Today, the civil parish embraces the ecclesiastical parishes of Witley and Milford and the northern part of Grayswood. In addition to these main villages, the parish also includes the hamlets of Moushill, Enton, Brook, Wormley, Sandhills, Stroud and Upper and Lower Birtley, with a total population approaching 7,500 people.

The Greensand Escarpment running eastwards from Brook, through Sandhills, and Wormley to Hambledon, divides the parish. To the south of the escarpment, the low undulating area of the Wealden Clays supports a number of small streams which flow from the higher ground below

Hindhead Common, eastwards, towards Chiddingfold. This drainage basin, which includes the Wareham Stream, supplies the headwaters of the River Arun.

To the north, in striking contrast, the soft sands of the Lower Greensand rise abruptly, to about 70m above the clays, the highest point being 152m above sea level, at Bannacle, above Sandhills; forming a distinctive ridge which provides some spectacular views to the south and east. The well-drained, unconsolidated, yellow sands dip gently to the north and a series of springs occur at their base, where these Hythe Beds meet the underlying Atherfield Clay. The few, small spring-fed streams, including the River Ock, drain to the north to meet the River Wey along the northern boundary of the parish. A band of hard sandstone, Bargate Stone, forms the high ground between Thursley, Witley and Enton, and provides a source of local building stone.

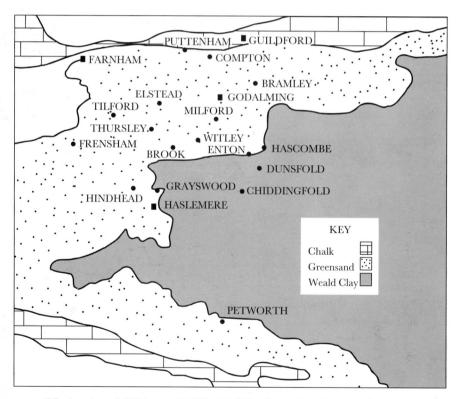

The location of Witley and Milford in West Surrey in relation to the geology.

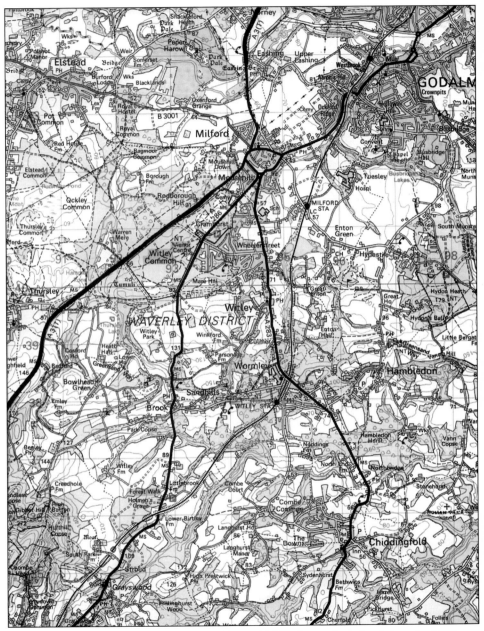

The location of the hamlets within the Witley and Milford area. Reproduced from the 1993, Sheet 183, 1:50,000 scale Ordnance Survey map by permission of Ordanance Survey Controller of Her Majesty's Stationery Office, © Crown Copyright MC 01000 30559.

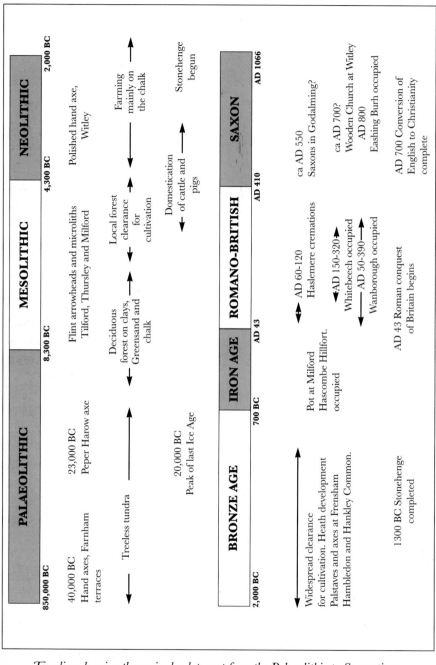

Timeline showing the main development from the Palaeolithic to Saxon times.

Chapter 1

Prehistoric Times to 1066

In the Beginning

The first evidence of human occupation in our area can be traced back to about 400,000 years ago, when the great ice sheets reached as far south as the River Thames. At that time the region now occupied by Witley Parish was treeless tundra with small, isolated ice caps on the hilltops. The ground was permanently frozen even in summer, so all water would run on the surface, carrying large amounts of gravel. The composition of these gravels, preserved in small isolated patches on Thursley Common and Hankley Common, show that the drainage pattern was very different and that the River Wey, which we see today to the west of Elstead, did not exist at that time.

It was some time before this coldest phase of the Ice Age, that primitive man wandered into our region, probably in search of food. This must have been a rich hunting ground, for he stayed in the area over a period of many thousands of years, making and losing stone artifacts. A large supply of flint hand axes and flakes have been found in the river terrace gravels at Farnham, some of which are about 120,000 years old. Gravels believed to be of the same age can be found along the River Wey at Elstead and at Oxenford. As the climate gradually improved, the ice retreated to the Midlands, and Palaeolithic man continued to enjoy the hunting in our region, leaving evidence in various forms, such as a small, sharp scraper with several mammoth teeth and bones of giant deer at Bramley, a broken hand axe at Frensham and a 23,000 year old axe at Peper Harow.

After a long period of cold and warm temperature fluctuations, by about 13,000 years ago, the climate began to improve. The tundra conditions, with permanently frozen ground, persisted as the ice caps slowly retreated northwards, so there were still considerable amounts of water destroying the land surface of Palaeolithic Man. This shifting drainage was eventually captured and diverted from supplying the River Blackwater south of Tilford, into the River Wey, to flow eastwards through Eashing and Godalming. Later still, the main headwaters of the River Blackwater which lay to the west, were captured by the River Wey at Farnham, and so formed the drainage pattern of the River Wey which we see today.

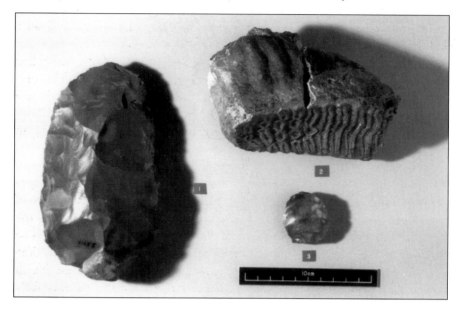

Palaeolithic implements. 1) Hand axe found in the terrace gravels at Farnham; 2) Mammoth tooth from Bramley and 3) Flint scraper, Bramley. Reproduced courtesy of Guildford Museum.

About 10,000 years ago, the climate suddenly improved and temperatures rose to about 3°C warmer than we experience today. Melting ice sheets caused a major rise in sea-level, to about 1-2 m higher than at present, and the land bridge connecting southern Britain to France was submerged. Improvements in climate saw the rapid development of the first deciduous forest, with the first juniper, birch, pine and hazel trees extending beyond the clay and Greensand areas, on to the chalk hills.

Heath Development at Thursley, Tilford and Witley

The boggy ground in the region of Pudmore Pond, between Thursley and Ockley Commons, provides one of the few sites in Britain which preserves pollens of the first vegetation to colonize the south of England after the Ice Age. From this, we can interpret the sequence of events associated with the first forest development and man's early settlement in our area.

The first trees to become established in the area were determined by the soil type and drainage, so there were mainly lime trees on the soils of the well-drained Lower Greensand and chalk. On the wetter, clay areas of the Weald, the dominant tree types were oak and elm, with willow and alder preferring the river valleys. Oak and elm also favoured the scarp of the Lower Greensand. This forestation took place at the start of the Mesolithic period. Around this time the first form of agriculture began. The first small-scale clearing and burning of forest produced localised heath and scrub in our area. This process continued intermittently over a few thousand years making the soil unsuitable for arable farming and resulting in the heath land, which characterizes our Greensand landscape today.

About 5,000 years ago, Neolithic man began to clear the forests more rigorously and to set out the first pastures, which still remain today. Clearance of the forest for the establishment of small areas of cultivation allowed the growth of hazel scrub, which provided an additional source of food. The deforestation of the chalk hills, particularly the South Downs, at this time was particularly drastic and continued into the Bronze Age. On the North Downs, superficial clay with flints meant the woodland was only fully cleared in the Iron Age and Roman periods.

The sudden decline in the population of elm trees in Britain about 5,000 years ago has been linked to the arrival of Neolithic agriculture. The bog pollens from the Thursley and Elstead area, show cereals and weeds appearing for the first time, and suggest a shifting pattern of clearance and crop cultivation within a predominantly wooded environment.

Deforestation is generally believed to be the cause of build-up of alluvium in river valleys and floodplains caused by soil erosion. In our area, there are significant alluvial deposits along the River Wey from Elstead to Eashing and in the small feeder streams which drain Ockley Common, and in the upper reaches of the River Ock at Wheeler Street, suggesting there might have been early deforestation and cultivation in the locality. Later in the Neolithic period, when the climate had deteriorated and the chalk hills were preferred for settlement, the forests returned to the Greensand areas.

By about 2,000 BC Bronze Age man, in improved climatic conditions, moved back to the area to resume cultivating the heathlands. The detailed pollen evidence from Elstead bog, together with flints, microliths and arrow heads of the Mesolithic and Neolithic Ages, indicate the long-term occupation of the loamy fertile soils of the Folkestone beds around Thursley and Tilford. Recently, some flints of the Mesolithic Age have been found at Milford Golf Course. From Neolithic times through the Bronze Age, settlement is inferred from pottery and metal tools including a palstave and two socketted axes found on Hankley Common.

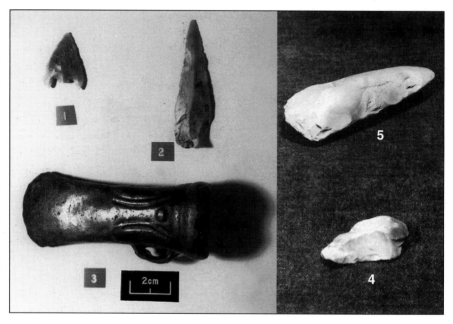

1) Mesolithic arrowhead, Frensham 2) Mesolithic flint microliths from Tilford,
3) Bronze Age palstave, Frensham. Reproduced courtesy of Guildford Museum.
4) Mesolithic scraper, Hambledon 5) Polished Neolithic hand axe, Witley.
Reproduced courtesy of Haslemere Educational Museum.

Other indications of Bronze Age occupation in the area include a palstave found at Frensham, another at Hambledon, and Bronze Age barrows at Chiddingfold, Witley, Thursley and Frensham. It seems, though, that the fertility of the soils was exhausted by this intensive use. This created the great expanses of heathland which have persisted to the present day. The remaining deciduous woodland on the chalk hills was removed, to allow even more development of pastoral grasslands. Elsewhere, areas of abandoned cultivation were colonised by beech, the last of the great trees to arrive. The result was the formation of the familiar chalk downland scenery which we see today.

Hascombe and the Early Iron Age

By the 8ᵗʰ century BC, the Iron Age was established, and average temperatures in Europe were about 1°C lower than at present and much wetter than before. Early man again moved away from the Witley area, leaving the Greensand regions clear of settlement, apart from the hillforts. The main occupation was again on the drier chalk regions and there is only scarce evidence of habitation in Milford during this time.

Perhaps the most interesting site locally is Hascombe Hillfort, dating from the later Iron Age, about 200 BC. This small fort is believed to have been a base for trade rather than defence, and for seasonal movement of livestock, known as transhumance, in this case grazing of pigs on the poor vegetation provided by the heathlands. There is archaeological evidence of trade in timber, quern stones from Petworth and Midhurst 25 km away and small-scale iron working. Cereals found at Hascombe Hillfort include emmer, spelt, six-rowed barley and oats. We might also suppose that Early Iron Age people lived in Milford as a fragment of a shouldered jar was found in the foundations of Hill House in 1954. This jar has been reconstructed and is displayed at Haslemere Educational Museum. The characteristic concave neck, flattened rim and finger-tip decorations are typical of Iron Age pottery in Southern England before 50 BC.

The inhabitants of the Witley area would have spoken a Celtic language until the arrival of the Anglo-Saxons. Evidence of this still survives in typical place-names, usually those relating to physical features such as rivers and streams, which are often preserved unaltered. Names which have been attributed by Eckert to a Celtic derivation include '*ock*' or '*oke*' and '*wey*' meaning water and are still associated with our local river names. Suggestions of early settlement in our area are preserved in place-names such as '*Rock House*' and '*Roke Manor,*' home of Alice atte Ok in 1332 and Richard atte Roke in 1389, now the site of Barrow Hills School, situated above a spring-fed tributary of the River Ock rising to the south of Barrow Hills School. Other spring-fed streams at Sweetwater and the Shadwell Brook also flow into the River Ock.

Reconstruction of the Early Iron Age jar found at Milford.
Reproduced courtesy of Haslemere Educational Museum.

Romano-British Influence in the Area

Although Julius Caesar arrived in Britain in 55 BC and again in 54 BC, Roman influence in the Weald area did not begin until much later, after the invasion by Claudius in AD 43. The region soon succumbed and there was never much Roman military presence here. Surrey remained divided, the Atrebatic tribe had their capital at Silchester, and the Cantiaci were based at Canterbury, with the boundary lying between the River Wey and the River Mole. One of the first priorities of the Romans was to improve the communication network, so by AD 50 the first of the great roads were constructed, from London to Silchester and from London to Chichester. A Roman road might once have existed in the Chiddingfold area to service the substantial Romano-British villa at Whitebeech, which was occupied between AD 150 and AD 320. This somewhat utilitarian building, by Roman standards, does not appear to have been associated with agricultural use, and archaeological evidence suggests it was probably the centre of a major forestry estate, exploiting the timber of the Weald. It may also have been a centre for the Wealden iron industry. The settlement included a religious outbuilding containing a bronze ibis dedicated to the god Isis. Baths and mosaic flooring, fragments of Spanish amphorae containing fish paste and oil, suggest that living conditions were very comfortable for the occupants.

Continuing occupation of earlier, British settlements, shows changes reflecting the increasing Roman influence in culture and in architectural style.

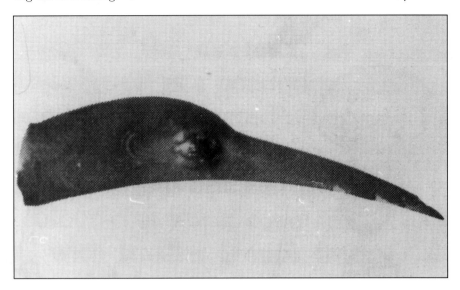

Bronze ibis found at the Whitebeech Romano-British villa near Chiddingfold.
Reproduced courtesy of Surrey Archaeological Society and John Gower.

This Romano-British culture was widespread, affecting all the ancient local settlements.

The temple dedicated to the Celtic god Jupiter at Wanborough indicates Romano-British occupation between AD 50 and the end of the 4th century AD, although the site was believed to have already been occupied in the Iron Age. Romano-British pottery and tiles found at this site were produced in the Alice Holt area and at Overwey, near Tilford. Evidence of a significant occupation in our locality is seen in the Romano-British burials at Tilford, Haslemere and Charterhouse, which are all cremations of an early date. At Haslemere, the burial site is an important 1st century and 2nd century cemetery containing twenty-six cremations in two groups which date from between AD 60 to AD 120.

7

Funerary pottery found in the Romano-British burials at Haslemere.
Reproduced courtesy of Haslemere Educational Museum.

The Saxons in and Around Witley

The Roman Empire was beset by numerous problems in the 4th century AD, and eventually the distant province of Britain was told to arrange its own defence. By the early 5th century the Saxons were invited in to protect the southern counties from invasion from the North and West. The South Saxons infiltrated Kent from Denmark, and the Frankish Saxons infiltrated from Southampton and spread northwards around the western edge of the Weald and beyond Winchester in the west. The early Saxon settlement was based around the Thames basin, and the south-west of Surrey seems to have been the last area of Surrey to come under Saxon control. Pagan Saxon burials have not been found, suggesting the Saxons were already Christian when they arrived, perhaps in the late 7th century. It used to be believed that once the Saxons were in control, the Celtic people in our area became isolated and either fled into the Weald forest, or were taken into slavery or killed. It is now more widely believed that the native Celtic population simply adapted to the culture of their new masters. They did this so thoroughly that, in time, they became indistinguishable. Eventually, by about AD 700, the Saxon Earls had control over all England.

Having taken over a once rich and fertile land where the social structure and monetary system had collapsed, the Saxons proceeded to develop the most advanced system of civil law, land administration and revenue collection in Europe at that time. Land was controlled by Earls and worked by freemen or sokemen, who represented the highest portion of the population. The subdivision of shires into 'Hundreds', and within them individual land holdings or manors, assisted the Saxon Kings in exerting considerable authority over the local lords, particularly when collecting substantial amounts of tax known as Danegeld, to finance the defence of the country against the marauding Danish.

The shire of Surrey was divided into 14 Hundreds. A 'Hundred' represented a group of 100 hides, a hide being a unit of land required to support one peasant family for a year. The term first appears in laws passed by King Edmund (AD 939-946). Each Hundred had a court to resolve private disputes and criminal matters. The court met once a month in the open air and at a time and place known to everyone. The court of the Godalming Hundred was held at the top end of Church Street, where the Pepperpot now stands.

The Godalming Hundred contained a number of distinct manors. Witley Manor, including Thursley and Grayswood, was one of these. The hamlet of Enton, however, lay within the Godalming Manor and so did Chiddingfold and Haslemere. Hambledon was a small separate manor, so was Peper Harow.

Witley Manor extended over Milford, Thursley, Stoatley and Grayswood. Until 1838, the Saxon chapel of Thursley was a chapelry to Witley. Witley was never incorporated within the Godalming court system, so Witley men only attended the Godalming Hundred court in disputes over ownership of land. The Manor of Witley was divided into four tithings: Milford including Moushill; Lea including Rokelands and Wheeler Street; Stoatley near Grayswood; Birtley including Brook and Sandhills.

The land around Godalming and Witley was owned by the King. In AD 880, Eashing was owned by King Alfred the Great and, in King Alfred's will, was named AEscengum after Aesci's people. The fortification at Eashing, listed in the Burghal Hideage of AD 920, is situated on the Bargate Sandstone cliff above the River Wey. The site was in use in King

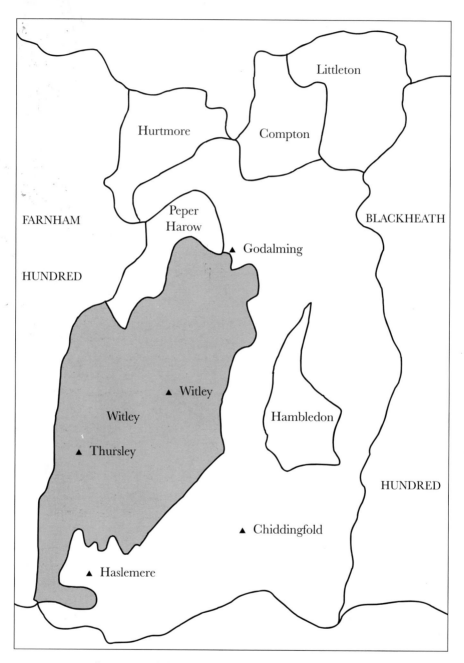

Saxon manorial holdings within the Godalming Hundred.
Based on the Domesday Survey.

Athelstan's reign and fell out of use following the development of Guildford. Historical evidence suggests only a short occupation of about 50 years, between AD 880 to AD 930.

In AD 685-8 a charter of the Saxon king of Wessex, Caedwalla, a newly converted Christian, granted an estate at Farnham, which coincides today with the Farnham Hundred, for the establishment of one of the first monastic estates in Britain, probably to obliterate the last remnants of paganism. Pagan burials, which had often been used to mark the territorial boundaries, now ceased. The link between these sites and current parish boundaries, suggests these early estates may have been established, at the latest, by the 6th century.

By about AD 700 the conversion of the Saxons to Christianity was complete and churches were being established throughout the country. Saxon churches at Witley and Godalming are recorded in the Domesday Book. The churches at Hambledon and Thursley indicate architectural evidence of their Saxon origins. The presence of a church is a clear indication of settlement in Witley at that time, although the homes were probably dispersed through the parish rather than clustered in the village.

By the end of the first millennium, Witley must have been sufficiently important to have a church and be included in the Domesday survey. The origin of the name 'Witley' is not known and could be the subject of exhaustive debate. The name has been attributed to various sources. Gover, Mawer and Stenton attribute the name to *'Witta's Leah'* where a '-leah' is a wood or clearing. Another possibility arises from a study of Professor Eckert's placename interpretations in which the Old English, *'Wiht'* could mean a bend in a hill or stream and *'–leah'* a glade used for religious purposes.

The bottom of Church Lane runs up a small valley, now occupied by the school and the Old Vicarage, but in living memory a small intermittent stream known locally as the River Wit would flow down Church Lane and past the church after heavy rain. We shall probably never know if this early church built by the Saxons was erected on the site of an even earlier pagan place of worship, as was so often the case during the conversion to Christianity.

11

The Saxons used the system of seasonal migration of stock, called trans-humance, for summer grazing in the Weald, as an important aspect of their life, reminiscent of the Iron Age practices of using outlying hillforts such as Hascombe. Clearings in the Weald areas were used for summer grazing and at this time placenames ending in '*–fold*' meaning 'a clearing for pasture' such as Chiddingfold and Dunsfold, begin to appear.

During the 9th century onwards for a few hundred years, the settled climate, with average summer temperatures warmer than today by about 1°C, pro-vided perfect conditions for extensive cultivation of the land. Arable land produced wheat, barley, oats and beans. Grain was milled, mainly by hand. Cloth was treated to remove the natural oils, by washing in a solution of Fullers Earth, a process assisted by the harnessing of water power. The River Wey and the River Ock were supporting six mills at Farnham, three at Godalming, one at Peper Harow and one at Hambledon by the time of Domesday, indicating a highly productive area at this time. Mills were com-monly sited in pairs, one on each side of the river, and were used for a variety of purposes. Changing use of mills in the historical records suggests their adaptation from fulling cloth to grinding corn and vice versa was fairly common.

Chapter 2

Domesday, the Middle Ages to 1599

Norman Influence

After the defeat of the Saxons at the Battle of Hastings in 1066, manorial land which had been previously owned by King Harold or his Earls, were reallocated to the Norman barons. Disagreement over territorial rights at this time meant that land was not cultivated or maintained as it had been, with the result that land holdings were less productive and reduced in value. The Norman barons took over a united kingdom of predominantly free-men, used to a highly developed social structure of law and order, land ownership and payment of dues. With the aim of maintaining law and order and, as far as possible, the productivity of the land, King William kept the Saxon language and the justice system and adopted the long-established land boundaries. The most fundamental and far reaching change was in land ownership. Now all land was deemed to belong to the king and he allocated estates by gift, to a relatively few barons, under tenancy agreements in exchange for their loyalty and duties at court. This meant that the Anglo-Saxon and Danish Earls, who had previously been freemen or 'sokemen', were now forced to become under-tenants, bound by service to a Norman baron.

In the Middle Ages, the manor was still the basic unit of landholding with its own court and probably its own hall, but not necessarily a manor house. Habitations in the late 11th century followed the ancient patterns of isolated farms, hamlets and tiny villages interspersed with fields and scattered over most of the cultivated land. Most houses, particularly in areas like Witley, where building stone was scarce, were flimsy affairs, made of a wooden frame with wattle and daub walls and reeds forming a roof. These houses were often destroyed by fire and provided very basic shelter.

The rudimentary nature of the common dwellings meant that settlements were capable of shifting over a period of time as local conditions varied.

.XXII.   TERRA GISLEBTI FILIJ RICHERIJ.

GISLEBERT fili Richerii
de Aigle ten WITLEI. Goduin tenuit . Tc se defd p xx.hid. Modo
p xii.hid.Tra.e.xvi.car.In dnio sunt.ii.car.7 xxxvii.uilli 7 iii.cot.
cu xiii.car. Ibi æccła.7 iii.ac prati.Silua.de xxx.porc.
T.R.E.7 post.ualb.xv.lib.Modo:xvi.lib

24 *   LAND OF GILBERT SON OF RICHERE

[In GODALMING Hundred] *
1 Gilbert son of Richere of L'Aigle holds WITLEY. Earl Godwin
held it. Then it answered for 20 hides, now for 12 hides.
Land for 16 ploughs. In lordship 2 ploughs;
    37 villagers and 3 cottagers with 13 ploughs. A church.
    Meadow, 3 acres; woodland at 30 pigs.
Value before 1066 and later £15; now £16.

*Domesday survey entry for Witley. Reproduced by kind permission from the Phillimore
edition of the Domesday Book (General Editor-John Morris) vol.3. Surrey. 1975.*

However, the boundaries of the parishes and large manors remained stable. Woodland made up only about 15% of the landscape, except for the Weald. During the 12th century the settlement on the Weald was based on clearings around summer pastures, so that villages such as Chiddingfold, Hambledon and Dunsfold grew up as groupings of farmsteads along an established road network and with no particular focus. Witley follows a similar pattern of isolated farmsteads with settlement developing along road intersections such as at Church Lane, Culmer and Wheeler Street, rather than at a particular focal point. This is in contrast to Godalming, which developed as a nucleated settlement, later to become a market town.

The Royal Manor of Witley

The Royal Manor of Witley was claimed by Gilbert Fitz-Richer de Aigle (meaning 'of the Eagle' and later to become latinised to 'd'Aquila') on behalf of his grandfather and father who fell at the Battle of Hastings. The yield of the land had fallen from 20 hides to 12 hides in the twenty years since the Conquest. There was land for 16 ploughs and it is estimated that a team of eight oxen could plough 1 hide or approximately 120 acres per year. In Witley, the villagers and cottars owned 13 ploughs and the lord held 2 ploughs, which means there could possibly have been about 120 oxen.

In 1086, this Royal Manor of Witley held 37 villagers (villains) which, including their families, probably amounted to around 185 people and three cottars (cottagers) i.e 15 people and no slaves. The population in Witley in 1086 was therefore about 200 people. The number of households would be something less than 40. The large proportion of villagers with the status of freemen with landholding, compared with the small number of cottagers who, although free, held little land, shows us that the settlement in the Manor of Witley was in the form of isolated farmsteads, rather than a nucleated settlement.

There were three acres of meadow, and woodland providing autumn feed for pigs. The assessment of 30 swine suggests that about 300 pigs were being grazed, as the Surrey assessment was 1 pig in ten. No mill is mentioned in the Manor of Witley.

Gilbert d' Aigle died in 1176 and his son, Gilbert, returned to Normandy with King Richard I and many other Norman landowners, to fight in the local baronial wars there in the late part of the 12th century. These wars continued in the reign of King John, until in 1204, Normandy was lost to Philip II of France. The d'Aigle family did not return to England and there was a long unsettled period when the custody of Witley Manor passed backwards and forwards between the monarch and various sheriffs. Gilbert d'Aigle died, presumably in Normandy, in 1231.

With the aim of pacifying his barons, Henry III began to create 'Honours,' consisting of a group of manors with power to hold a court which had civil and criminal jurisdiction. King Henry III granted the 'Honour of Aquila' and Lordship of the Manor of Witley to Gilbert Marshall, Earl of Pembroke, in 1234 until Gilbert's untimely death in a jousting tournament in 1241. Peter of Savoy, Queen Eleanor's uncle, was created Earl of Richmond in 1241 and given the Lordship of Witley Manor in a ceremony designed to raise the profile of, and to attract young recruits into, the knighthood. It is at about this time that the name changed from the old family name of 'd'Aigle' to 'd'Aquila'. The manor retained the name 'Aquila' long after the family had claims to Witley.

Witley now held its own court. On such occasions the lord or his Steward received homage and held his 'view of frankpledge'. This is when households of each tithing gave pledges for the good behaviour of each other, twice a year, once after Easter and once after Michelmas. It is not known for certain if there was a courthouse, or where it was situated, but in the 16th century, the manor house owned by the king was reputed to have been in the vicinity of the north-east of the churchyard in Witley. By the time of the survey of King Edward VI in 1547, the house might no longer have been standing, if indeed the courts had taken place in a building at all. This might be supposed because Thomas Jones, gentleman and Kings Steward of the Manor of Witley held

> *'at farm from year to year, the site of the Manor there with demesne closes, land and pasture next to the same site containing by estimate 20 acres called le Corteland.'*

In the documentation of a dispute between Thomas Jones and John Mellershe in 1576, a 'Queen's Manor house of Witley near the church there' is referred to.

However, at this time, in the early 14th century, the family of le Court were the main landowners. They lived at Moushill and were known to have held Courts Baron in the time of Henry V.

Between 1258 and 1265, there was widespread local unrest in England when the barons tried to revolt against King Henry III and his French advisors. The creation of 'Honours' was a means of appeasing the English Barons, who were dissatisfied with his weak rule and were seeking greater powers over their lands. As the king demanded greater revenues from his barons to replenish the Crown's impoverished coffers, following prolonged wars of previous monarchs and to support his lavish lifestyle, Peter of Savoy raised the rents in Witley. The local people protested, and this unhappy time for the inhabitants of Witley Manor continued until his death in 1264.

King Edward I took control of the manor on the death of his father in 1272 and later bestowed it on his mother, the Dowager Queen Eleanor. She released her tenants from the oppressive taxes of her predecessor, on condition that they hold an annual service in Witley church for the souls of her husband and for Peter of Savoy. Queen Eleanor died in 1291 and the Lordship of the manor of Witley passed back to the Crown. Following the civil unrest during his father's reign, Edward I was concerned to restore control over England, and his tenants in chief in particular. He made many royal progresses through his royal manors. On 25th June 1294, King Edward I spent the night at Witley on his way to Portsmouth and issued documents from his Court at Witley. Again between 8th and 12th June 1305, he held Court at Witley. King Edward I died in 1307 and probably at this time, the manor passed to his wife, the Dowager Queen Margaret.

On 29th July 1324, the weak and unpopular King Edward II visited Witley. After he was deposed and murdered in 1327, his widow, Queen Isabella, held the manor of Witley. For three years she and her lover governed England until, in 1330, the young King Edward III rebelled and imprisoned his mother for the rest of her life. The manor of Witley then went to Queen Philippa in 1333. On her death in 1369, the King granted a lease of the Manor of Witley to Andrew Tyndale, his valet, for life.

This was a difficult period in England, and Witley was no exception. In the wake of the Black Death and having to endure the effects of the Statute of Labour and the Poll Tax of 1381, there was considerable unrest in the

Surrey countryside. The situation in Witley was aggravated by the fact that, in 1377, the eleven year old King Richard II, on the advice of the regent, his uncle John of Gaunt, Duke of Lancaster (whose emblem was the Red Lion), granted the manor of Witley to his French nurse Mundina Danos and her husband Walter Rauf for life. In the years that followed they were not popular, as they tried to extract their dues from the men of Witley.

In 1388-89, they accused a group of tenants of breaking into the warren over a period of three years, removing 40 rabbits and 6 hares and destroying the warren. For this and other infringements of their duties as tenants, Stephen le Erl, Alan of Milford, William Rede of Moushill and Richard Roke were committed to the prison of the King's Marshelsea. Three others, William Heggere, William Hameldon and Richard Goos, who had failed to attend their trial, were later apprehended and imprisoned.

Richard II, whose emblem was the White Hart, retained his royal hunting lodge in Witley, and this is believed to have been Asshehurst Manor in Witley Deer Park, which he ordered to be restored after rioters broke in during 1379.

Richard II was imprisoned in 1399 by Henry Bollingbroke, son of John of Gaunt, Duke of Lancaster and grandson of Edward III. Bollingbroke was proclaimed King Henry IV, the first Lancastrian King.

In 1402, under Henry IV, the men of Witley obtained a charter exempting them from contributing to the knights of the shire, as tenants of the crown, or from serving on juries. (This charter was later confirmed by Queen Elizabeth I in 1574.) Henry V succeeded his father to the throne in 1413. However in 1422, Henry V died suddenly of dysentery, whilst fighting for the crown of France, and left a baby of nine months old to inherit the crown.

England was governed from 1422 to 1447 by the Duke of Gloucester, Earl of Pembroke, who was the uncle to Henry VI, and Witley was granted to John Feriby, the King's clerk, for life. We hear very little of Witley until after Gloucester's imprisonment and death in 1447 by Margaret of Anjou, wife of Henry VI. In 1453, Henry VI granted the Lordship of the Manor of Witley to his half-brother Jasper Tudor, Earl of Pembroke. England finally conceded defeat to the French in the Hundred Years War and Henry VI became insane for a short time, which provided Richard Duke of York with the opportunity to become regent.

Later, with the death of Henry VI during the Wars of the Roses, the House of Lancaster was eventually deposed by Richard of York in 1460, who was himself killed the same year before being proclaimed king. His son Edward IV became king in 1461 and transferred the Lordship of Witley Manor from Jasper, Earl of Pembroke, to his uncle who also immediately died. King Edward IV then granted Witley to his brother George, Duke of Clarence. However in 1478, Parliament condemned George for plotting against the King. He was imprisoned in the Tower of London where he died, drowned in a 'butt of malmsey'. In Witley Church, on the north side of the wall in the sanctuary, is a half-finished inscription to George, Duke of Clarence, Lord of the Manor of Witley and brother of Edward IV.

When Henry VII won the crown for the Tudors in 1485, he restored Witley to his uncle Jasper, the Earl of Pembroke, who was presumably an old man by that time.

On 11th May 1544, during the reign of Henry VIII, the stewardship of the Manor of Witley including Witley Deer Park, was granted to Thomas Jones, son of the food taster, or 'Server of the Chamber' to the King, who had died in 1525 and is buried in Witley Church. His son, Thomas Jones the younger, was granted the Stewardship of the Royal Manor of Witley for life. He farmed Sattenham near Rake and amassed a large estate in Witley before he died in 1597. He also farmed the site called le Corteland, which was owned by the King. He constructed a fishpond on the borders of Witley and Thursley parishes, now known as Forked Pond.

Perhaps Thomas Jones is best known for the action he brought against John Mellershe, miller and owner of Rake Mill in 1576. Jones accused Mellershe of flooding his land and of unlawfully using a private road across his land at Sattenham, which led from the courthouse near the church at Witley over the fields to Sattenham to the fulling mill at Rake. The local men who gave evidence to support Mellershe recalled the lane running from the highway from Witley and Thursley to Chisbury Hatch, then on through Fulmer Field to Rake Mill and over a field called Old Sattenham Field into Milk Lane. The local inhabitants had been accustomed to using this lane and did not recall any right of way being challenged *'until the time of the general rebellion in these parts, when the pale of the Queen's Majesty's Park of Witley was pulled down.'*

From these comments, we might suppose there was some considerable local opposition to the enclosure of the Deer Park and that the Queen's Steward sought reprisal by means of his action against Mellershe.

Mellershe also owned a house at Dyttons in Wheeler Street at the cross-roads which later became known as Dittons Corner. After the court action, Dyttons was mortgaged to pay costs; the family was eventually bankrupt and had to leave Rake and Wheeler Street.

After Thomas Jones died in 1597, the Lord of the Manor, Sir Edward Fynys, Lord Clinton and Saye, exercised his option to sell the estate. The estate was sold to Sir George More of Loseley, who then kept the area of Witley Park and the heaths around Thursley and Witley and sold off the lordship of the manor with the remaining land to Henry Tanner, alias Bell, of Godalming.

Witley Deer Park

Although the Park was not named in the Domesday survey of Witley, there are records of a Royal Park here in the early 13th century. In 1271 it was mentioned as owned by the Crown, and in 1294 and 1299 King Edward 1 visited Witley, possibly to hunt. In 1313, Queen Margaret sent five massive oaks from Witley Park for the King's Great Hall at Westminster.

At the southern end of Witley Deer Park was a moated farmstead. Moated sites were built between 1200 to 1325 and appear to have been an indication of status, which declined after the Black Death. There are about 150 moated sites in Surrey, most on the Weald Clay. Our site, at the present South Park, occupied four acres within Witley Deer Park and consisted of a moated house, woodland and spring-fed pond. Enclosing the house and out-buildings, the system of moats was not necessarily a defensive structure but had a dual purpose to improve drainage at a time when the climate was deteriorating, and to rear fish.

There was a long period of earlier settlement here, from the Mesolithic and Bronze Ages and later to Saxon and Norman times (ca 900 to 1100). This later became the site of the small royal manor of Asshehurst and later the keeper's lodge of Asshehurst Park. The moats were constructed between 1150 and 1400. Pottery dating from 1300 to 1350 indicates occupation at this time and Asshehurst Manor was first documented in 1313 when Henry de Guildeford held it from Queen Margaret, who also owned the Royal Manor of Witley. In 1378, Philip Walwayn the Elder, Usher of the King's Chamber, was granted the manor of Asshehurst and park for life. But this lordship did not appear to be popular with the local population for, in 1379,

> *'malefactors and disturbers of the peace broke into our (the King's) park of Asshehurst bearing arms and unlawfully hunted, killed, seized and carried away the deer therein and threatened the Parker in his lodge so he feared for his life.'*

In 1385, the King commanded Philip Walwayn and William Tailliard to take sufficient masons, carpenters and labourers to repair the King's Manor of Asshehurst at the King's cost.

King Edward IV granted the Park in 1463 to his brother, the Duke of Clarence, who also owned Witley Royal Manor. At this time the two were amalgamated and Asshehurst became part of Witley Manor. It is believed that the moated site was abandoned by the end of the 15th century and no remains were left by the middle of the following century.

In a survey of the manor of Witley by King Edward VI in 1547 to 1549, there was no mention of the moated site. At this time there was nothing but fallow deer in the 900 acre park and the value was assessed as nil because of this. By this time the Keeper of the Park was Thomas Jones, who was based at Sattenham, near the village of Witley.

By 1596, the park was only 400 acres or three miles in circumference and there were only 100 deer. Thomas Jones died in 1597 and soon afterwards, in 1599, the estate was sold to the More family of Loseley. The next time the park was assessed, it was valued in terms of the iron ore it produced and there were no deer. By 1788, when the iron industry had all but ceased in this area, the park had been divided into farms and turned into arable land.

Reconstruction of the moated farmhouse at South Park. Reproduced courtesy of Surrey County Archaeological Unit. Drawing by Giles Pattinson.

Manors Adjoining Witley Manor

Oxenford and Links with Waverley Abbey

The 11th and 12th centuries saw the major period of cathedral building throughout the country, and also in France and Spain. Here in the adjoining Hundred of Farnham, the Cistercian order established Waverley Abbey in 1128. This was the first Cistercian Abbey founded in England. The monks of Waverley Abbey are believed to be responsible for building the series of medieval bridges spanning the River Wey between Farnham and Guildford, including Elstead and Eashing bridges. These bridges are mentioned in documents dated 1223. They were responsible for introducing from France the practice of breeding large numbers of sheep, which not only denuded the landscape but provided the fleeces which established the early clothing industry and associated fulling mills in the area.

In 1147, Gilbert d'Aigle granted lands at Oxenford in the northern part of Witley Manor to the newly established Waverley Abbey. According to a charter under the Honour of d'Aquila in 1309, the tenants of Oxenford farm in Witley Manor, like the other men of Witley, were allowed as many animals in the common pasture of Witley during summer as they wintered on their own holding.

The land remained within Waverley Abbey until the Dissolution of the Monasteries by King Henry VIII in 1536. Then the lands were divided, some included in the grant of the site of Waverley Abbey to Sir William Fitz William, master of the Royal Hunt, and then to Sir Anthony Browne, who became the 1st Viscount Montague, who died in 1592. His son, Sir Henry Browne, sold the lands to Sir George More of Loseley in 1609.

It is believed that much of the building stone for Loseley House came from the ruined Waverley Abbey. The part within Witley known as Oxenford, with 120 acres, fell into the possession of the Countess of Southampton. Oxenford Grange was demolished in 1775, to be used for the new mansion house at Peper Harow Park. The architect, Pugin, was employed by the 5th Viscount Middleton to build an imitation 13th century farm on the land in Witley parish.

Peper Harow and Hurtmore

Adjoining Witley manor to the north and within the Hundred of Godalming, was the small Peper Harow manor, with about 35 inhabitants in 1086, seven acres of meadow and a mill. Previously owned by King Edward the Confessor, Peper Harow was now held by Walter son of Othere, founder of the House of Windsor and Keeper of the Royal Forests of Berkshire. Walter held the small adjacent manor of Hurtmore, which included a mill and six acres of meadow.

Godalming Manor

King Edward the Confessor had also owned the Godalming Manor. Then, after the Conquest, the manor passed to William I. In 1086, the Godalming Manor probably consisted of about 500 people. Of these, a small group of about 36 people lived at Tuesley, where there was a Saxon minster church dedicated to the blessed virgin. The place-name Tuesley contains a reference to the Pagan god 'Tiw', and this may suggest that the minster church was deliberately established here to replace a pagan temple. The minster at Tuesley was later entirely replaced by the church of Saints Peter and Paul at Godalming. The land attached to this church was also assessed separately in the Domesday survey as having around 85 occupants.

The rest of the Godalming Manor held about 400 people, with only two slaves. At 24 hides, the area was only slightly more productive than Witley, yet the value of £25 to £30 suggests the produce was of much higher economic value. The 25 acres of meadow and three mills, valued at 41s. 8d, would have contributed to this prosperity.

It is not proven where these mills were sited, but they would have been water-powered, as windmills did not appear in England until the end of the 12th century. Some scholars believe the mills to be Hatch Mill, Catteshall Mill and possibly Enton Mill or Rake Mill. We know, according to Domesday, that there were six mills in the Farnham Hundred and six mills in the Godalming Hundred. Of these, three mills were in the Godalming Manor, one mill at Hurtmore, one at Peper Harow and one at Hambledon. The exact location of the Saxon mills has not been proved and is the subject of debate. Wherever the Saxon mills were located, it is known for certain that the period from 11th century to the 15th century saw considerable expansion of the milling industry in the area, interrupted only by the Black Death and based originally on grinding corn, then for fulling of woollen cloth. During the Middle Ages we know that, in our area alone, there were three mills on the River Wey, at Eashing, Westbrook and Catteshall, and three on the River Ock at Enton, Rake and Hatch Mill in Godalming. It is believed that Ockford Mill on the River Ock was built in the 19th century, although a pond 'Hock Water' is shown on early maps.

Hambledon Manor

King Edward the Confessor owned the Hambledon Manor, and this passed to Edward of Salisbury after the Conquest, but was held by Ranulf Flambard, also the under-tenant to the King, for Godalming. Hambledon, although a tiny manor of a few hundred acres, had a population of 58, which included 13 slaves, and a mill. It is not clear where this mill would have been sited, the best streams being those draining the dip-slope of the Greensand escarpment. The unusually large number of slaves in this small manor suggests the economy was not entirely based on agriculture, but might have been associated with some local industry. The close proximity of the ancient Romano-British site at Whitebeech might suggest the possibility of continuing industrial activity, probably based on locally derived iron-ore extraction and smelting. Some iron cinder has been found at the Whitebeech site but the archaeological evidence of glass manufacture is apparently less compelling.

Agriculture and Growth of Settlements

During this Early Medieval time, the warm climate provided ideal conditions for the growth and development of agriculture. Average summer temperatures were about 1°C warmer than at present and grapevines could again be cultivated in England.

The main sources of meat at this time were pigs and fish, supplemented by the occasional rabbit or hare. Sheep were plentiful but the breed, much smaller than we are familiar with today, was used mainly for the fleece in the manufacture of woollen cloth, and the skins used for making parchment and other leather goods. Salt was the main means of preservation but it was scarce and therefore valuable. It was produced mainly from salt pans on the coast and from mines in Cheshire and Worcestershire. Salters' carts were a feature on the roads during the Middle Ages and probably passed through our area from Hascombe towards Farnham along Salt Lane at Hydestile. Pepper and spices were valuable and the term 'Peppercorn' rent dates from this time when men were glad to take rent in pepper. Freshwater fish such as pike, roach, bream, dace, and eels and lamphreys were necessary for the fast-days and to supplement meat.

Honey was important for sweetening and *'Inbeham'*, now Imbhams near Haslemere, was named in 1202 and is believed to be derived from *'Emley'*, which is an Old English name for 'swarm of bees' or 'place where the bees swarm'.

Increasing prosperity and trade brought a strengthening monetary system gradually replacing barter and saw the development of market towns. The ability to hold a market was a privilege only granted by the lord, so it must have been a major event in the life of the local inhabitants when, on 30th April 1283, King Edward I granted a weekly market to Witley:

> *'To the Sheriff of Surrey. Order to cause a Proclamation to be made in his County Court, of a market at the Manor of Whitelye, which Queen Eleanor the King's mother holds in Dower, on Friday in every week and to cause the markets to be held, as the King wills that a market shall be held there for ever.'*

After a period of notably warm dry summers, the climate changed abruptly, when a run of wet summers was followed by wet springs and autumns. This poor weather continued until about 1321, causing poor harvests in Britain and northern Europe, leading to famine, disease and deaths. Large numbers of sheep and cattle died in epidemics which swept the sodden and often flooded land.

Following a sudden hot spell in 1348, the Black Death arrived. This Bubonic Plague, carried by infected rats, spread from southern England; also at about this time St Anthony's Fire, caused by blackened kernels of rye in damp harvests, was common. In the latter half of the 14th century, living conditions were so bad throughout the country, that life expectancy was reduced by 10 years. There were severe consequences in terms of harvests not gathered in, labour shortages and rising costs. These famine years saw a reduction in the population in the 14th century with devastating effects on the local communities, agriculture and local industries. In some areas this resulted in abandonment of settlements. It might be that Asshe-hurst manor was abandoned at about this time, sometime in the early or mid 15th century. This episode brought in a change in agriculture and land-holding and many farmsteads and mills changed hands.

In 1351, the imposition of The Statute of Labour meant that even though the shortage of labour resulted in crops not being harvested, labourers' wages were curbed and kept to the level of the pre-Black Death times. At about the same time, Richard II was imposing heavy taxes to pay for the excesses of the Hundred Years War with France (1337-1453). Local unrest flared up around the country and Witley was no exception. In 1376 there was a threat, issued from the Bishop of Winchester, nailed to the door of Witley Church against

'certain sons of perdition, with machines, snares, nets, dogs, bows and arrows and other mysteries, who had carried off, to the great peril of their souls, rabbits and other wild beasts'

from Farnham Park.

Surrey was one of the main counties which took part in the Peasants' Revolt in 1381. Could the burning of heath at Geradeswod (Grayswood) and at Wormele (Wormley), that Justice of the Peace Richard of Medemefeld and others were sworn to investigate in 1380-81, have been connected with those troubles?

Following the Black Death, nucleation and growth of the towns was reflect-ed on a smaller scale in the villages. Improvements in building techniques, including the use of brick, meant that houses were more substantially con-structed and provided better protection against the deteriorating weather conditions. The result was that more permanent settlement patterns emerged. The earliest surviving form of domestic dwelling from this time is the 'hall-house'. These simple houses had two or more bays, open to the roof with no upper floor. These are now often incorporated into larger, more recent dwellings. Slightly larger houses of three bays in length might have had one end floored over and a single bay in the centre.

We see evidence for this settlement development in our area in the ancient houses dating from the 13th century and 14th century at Rake, Moushill and

Sattenham for example, even though in many cases little or nothing remains of the original building. *Mushulle* or 'mouse infested hill' was first recorded in the Assize Rolls in 1236, when the Family of le Court who were the chief landowners, lived there. In 1303, Richard le Court and his wife Alice bought rights in a moor and appurtenances lying somewhere between

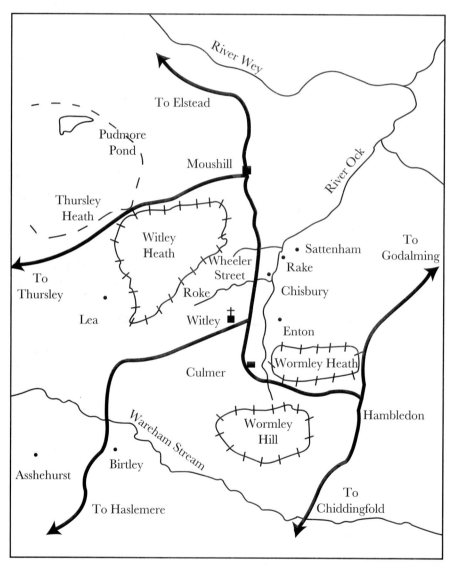

Settlements in the 13th and 14th centuries

Robert Asshehurst's land (Witley Park area) and Richard le Court's land in Witley. By 1323, Alice had left her husband and, relinquinshing her rights to their jointly held lands, was now known as Alice atte Leye. In 1324, Richard le Court bought Rake Mill, all lands, tenements and appurtenances in the Parish of Witley from Richard de Medemefelde, son of Robert de Rake. Richard le Court must have remarried, for in 1335, his widow, Cecily, leased land at Moushill Manor to Thomas atte Dene and Robert, son of John le Court, who was possibly a nephew of Richard le Court. This Robert le Court then leased the mill 'enclosed on every side in Wittele for life paying 3/- per year' to Robert le Muleward of Thorsele.

Robert Court held Court Baron for the Manor of Moushill early in the reign of Henry V (1413–1422). The estate later passed by marriage into the Shudd family, who also owned Cosford. The manor of Court Thorn, or Moushill Manor, passed to the Stillwell family of Thursley by marriage. In 1701, John Stillwell held the last Court Baron there. The manor remained in the Stillwell family until about 1822, when it was bought by the Viscount Middleton of Peper Harow.

Within Witley and Milford old houses, which are most probably based on even older settlements, include The White Hart public house, Church Steps Cottage and Step Cottage, which is early 16th century but based on an earlier hall-house. Red Rose cottages are possibly a medieval Hall-house of the 15th century, they were certainly built by the late 16th century.

One of the earliest records of local places appears in 1235 when *Muleford* is interpreted as Milford. The mill is probably Rake Mill, a fulling mill owned by Richard at Rake before 1324. The origin of the name 'rake' is unknown, but it has been linked with the old English word *'thrace'* meaning 'throat', or it might be derived from the old English word *'ak'* meaning 'oak' and pronounced *ayk*. The 'R' might be derived from the common practice of including in the place name the description *'ate there'* or 'at the' when the last syllable becomes part of the succeeding place name. This might also have happened with the name Roke where we have early references to Alice atte Ok.

Sattenham was recorded in the Ministers Accounts in 1303; Lower Birtley was the home of John de Berkleye in 1332; Lea farm, or Lye in 1332, was the home of Adam atte Leye; Wormley was first mentioned in 1340.

Chisbury, one of the earliest settlements in Witley, was the home of Richard de Chesburgh in 1210, five years before the Magna Carta in the reign of King John. The Chisbury property consisted of farmland with about fifty acres of arable, meadow, common pasture, woodland and orchard. In 1310, Wytley Chesberries was described as the 'small manor of William de Chussebury de Muleford'. This suggests that the earliest settlement of Muleford might possibly have been situated in the vicinity of Rake, and that the village settlement which we see today might be based on a post 15th century development. Further study of the early manuscripts might provide a definite view on this.

Enton fell within the royal manor of Godalming, and the name could possibly, based on Eckert, be derived from the Anglo Saxon word *'tun'* meaning fence or enclosure, combined with *'Ing'* meaning the outlying settlement of the Ingas of Godalming. Alternatively, Gover, Mawer and Stenton suggest the name is derived from *'Eningtun'* meaning 'Eni's farm.' Whichever you prefer, William of Enyton lived there sometime between 1309 and 1339 with his wife Julia. In 1332, Julia was fined relating to a messuage and lands in Chiddingfold.

At the southern end of Witley, beneath Wormley Hill, lay Culmer Farm first mentioned as Conemere in 1332. Lower Birtley, Roke and Lea Farm were first mentioned at this time. Culmer, consisting of about 100 acres of farm and heath, was a significant landholding about the same size as Chisbury and Roke.

Wheeler Street was the settlement along the main road at either side of Dittons Corner and on Wheeler Lane. It is believed to be named after a local family; one of its early members was Nicholas Whelere (1373). This family might have been spinners, as Wheeler Street was an important junction linking the fulling mill at Rake with the road to Thursley, Elstead and Farnham.

Land to the south of Wheeler Street was known as Rokeland. Roke Lane, even as late as 1768, was no more than a track leading to Rock Farm on the edge of Witley Common. In 1389, Richard atte Oke occupied Roke and possibly so did his antecedent Alice atte Ok in 1332. Roake, or Rokeland, was held by Walter, son of John Roke in 1548. Thomas Clarke sold Rokelands and Roke House to Thomas Carrill in 1585. Six years later it went to John Westbrook for 100 years. In 1764, Richard and William Westbrook sold the land to Thomas Smith of Witley.

All Saints Church, Witley

A church in Witley is mentioned in the Domesday survey and was almost certainly to have been on the site of the present All Saints' Church. The first building was most likely to have been a wooden structure. Although there is no known archaeological evidence to suggest this, the wooden church may have been built at the time of conversion of the area to Christianity, and placed on an earlier pagan site. It could therefore be possible that the first Christian church may have been built here in about AD 680.

The first stone building on the site has been argued, by some, to predate the Conquest. However, a study in 1981 by David Park of the Courtauld Institute of Art, London, showed that the Saxon style windows in the south side of the nave were probably contemporary with the early walls and the Norman doorway. Additional evidence of a post-Conquest date for the walls is provided by the wall paintings, which were painted on the first layer of plaster. Architectural evidence therefore supports the view that the first stone building dated from the first third of the 12th century. Although Witley church is a relatively humble building, this date coincides with an extensive period of church building across Britain, Northern Europe and most of the Christian world. It will be remembered that Waverley Abbey was also constructed at about this time.

The original building consisted of the nave with a door in the south side. The cruciform shape was created by the addition of a tower, chancel and two transepts in about 1180, during Henry II's reign. About 100 years later, the Manor Chapel was added, coinciding with the declaration of Queen Eleanor, that Witley men should pray on a set day each year for the souls of Peter of Savoy and the late King Henry III, her husband. Could it be that she paid for the chapel, and is the day of prayer still observed? Fragments of a rare medieval stained glass window are preserved in the north wall of the Manor Chapel. One fragment represents the Royal Arms of the Plantagenet Kings, and one represents the arms of a French prince, probably Peter of Savoy, married to an English princess. The church contains a wealth of interesting features reflecting the local history but it is not possible to include a description of this or the rectory manor in this volume.

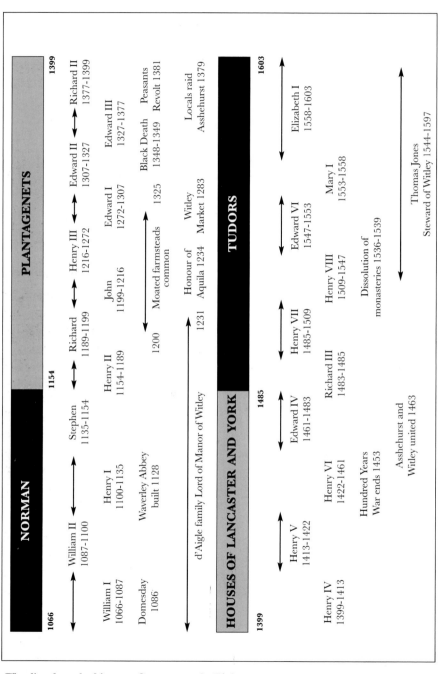

Timeline from the Norman Conquest to the Tudors

Chapter 3

Social and Industrial Development to 1800

Social Change During the 16ᵗʰ and 17ᵗʰ Centuries

Towards the end of the 16th century the crown sold off large amounts of its manorial lands, and the Royal Manor of Witley was sold in 1599 after the death of the Steward and Keeper of the Park, Thomas Jones. The lands including the deer park, which due to its non-productive use had been valued in 1547 at £0, were bought by Sir George More of Loseley. He also bought Oxenford and the Godalming Manor at about the same time.

The More family built the iron works on the heath between Thursley and Witley Commons sometime early in the new century, and these are commonly believed to be the last iron works to be built in Surrey. In May 1610, Sir George More and Sir Robert More leased the ironworks and split the Witley estate. The land around Witley and Milford, along with the lordship of the old royal manor of Witley, was sold to Henry Bell, Clerk Controller to King James, in 1614 for £1,100. Henry Bell had bought Rake Mill in 1592 from the Mellershe family, after they left Rake in 1591. Henry Bell had the house rebuilt over a period of thirty years, before he moved in. In 1618/19, Bell and Sir Robert More set up a rabbit warren on Thursley Heath at Warren Mere and built a house for the warrener. Then in 1622, Henry Bell bought the fishpond called 'Forked Pond', which Thomas Jones had constructed on the borders of Witley and Thursley from the More family. In 1623 Henry Bell, now described as 'of Milford', bought the ironworks for £200.

By 1629 Bell also owned Sattenham, Court House, Witley meadows, called Lordes Meade and Pond Meade, lands called Beadle Landes, and land in Milford. Henry Bell died at his house in Milford, believed to be Rake, in 1634 aged about 80. The inscription on his memorial in Witley Church reads:

> 'Here lies interred the body of Henry Bell, Esquire late Clarke Controwler of the Household to our late Soveraigne Lord King James of blessed memorie, who departed this mortall life on the 1Xth of May 1634 at his house in Milford in

Surrey & aged 80 yeares or there about, & was buried ye 13 day of ye same moneth, & here he rests in hope of a joyfull resurrection.'

As he was unmarried, Rake passed to Bell's great nephew, Anthony Smith (jr) and his wife Joan Hoare of Farnham. The Smiths lived at Rake as Lord of the Manor of Witley for 40 years. A cast-iron fire back, dated 1630 and made at Thursley to the standard works pattern, commemorates their move to Rake in 1629.

Coat of Arms of Anthony Smith. Reproduced courtesy of Godalming Museum.

Anthony Smith was a country gentleman and the historical records suggest he believed in preserving the countryside from the ravages of the local population. He had taken over the ironworks in April 1634, shortly before Henry Bell's death. He leased the ironworks, now called Horsebane Hammer, but retained the fishing rights to the carp in the hammer ponds. After the Dissolution of the Monasteries in the 16th century, a fish diet had been prescribed as a relic of an ancient rule going back to the Middle Ages. In the reign of Queen Elizabeth I, there were 145 fish days each year and long after her reign, the fish in the hammer ponds of Surrey were considered to be a valuable asset.

During Henry Bell's ownership the Pudmore area had been drained to allow the local tenants to cut peat as a cheap source of fuel. However, there was a scarcity of wood for household use caused by the demand for fuel for ironworks and, before that, the local glass making industry in the Chidding-fold area. People were now travelling from as far away as Hindhead to cut peat on Pudmore. Anthony Smith made many protests about this. It was eventually agreed at a Court Baron in 1634, involving all the local tenants with familiar names such as Thomas and William Shudd, Henry Roker, Henry Stovall, John Stillwell, Richard Stillwell, and Edmund Yalden, that peat cutting should be restricted to the immediate tenant farmers of land, and limited to 10,000 turves of peat cut and dried, to be supplied by Anthony Smith for 3 shillings the thousand, and that no peat should be taken away and sold, either by the lord or tenant.

In the years preceding the Civil War, there was increasing unease between the local tenants and the landed gentry. By 1635, the problems caused by poachers in the Witley area were so bad, that Anthony Smith called for royal support, but this was a long time coming. It was not until 1665/6, that Charles II commanded Smith to be responsible for game preservation and royal hunting rights within an eight-mile radius of his house at Witley. He was ordered

'to preserve the hare, pheasant, partridge, heath poult, heron and other wild fowl, much destroyed by divers disorderly persons'.

Smith also had trouble at this time with the tenancy of his ironworks. Francis Wyatt from Redsall in Puttenham had leased the

'forge or ironworks called Horsebane Hammer and one furnace and ironwork then newly erected and set up near the said forge all situate and lying in Witley Heath and Thursley Heath'

in 1634 for seven years at the rate of £40 per year. This was a much lower rent than previous contracts and might reflect the fact that Anthony Smith retained access to the area for fishing his carp in the ponds. Anthony Smith also agreed to provide Francis Wyatt 10,000 turves of peat to be delivered to the ironworks at the rate of twelve pence per thousand.

All seemed to go well in the agreement with Wyatt. However, shortly after taking up the leasehold, Francis Wyatt died suddenly and the leasehold passed to his wife Tymothy. However, shortly after taking over, she also died. The ironworks were then taken over and run by Thomas and John Burrell who claimed to be the executors of the Wyatts, and we can assume from the later court actions that Anthony Smith was not happy with this arrangement. It was towards the end of this lease that arguments broke out over the restocking of the fish in the Finery Pond and the Hammer Pond. Anthony Smith had apparently been exercising his fishing rights and was accused of failing to fulfill his obligation to restock the ponds and thereby, supposedly, denying the tenants rights to a share of the fish stocks. We shall probably never know if this was due to problems with local poachers or if it was a ploy to remove his tenant ironmaster, for in 1639, Smith was accused of removing a *'Penstock or 'ingine' from one of the hammer ponds.'* This was supposed to have drained the pond and made it useless for the ironworks. Smith was fined damages of £40.

Pudmore Pond, part of Thursley Nature Reserve, with the site of the Thursley ironworks in the middle distance.

Smith was also accused of breaking this agreement to supply turves of peat for the ironworks and of removing iron sows to the value of £40. Smith pleaded not guilty in October 1641.

In his defence, Smith claimed the turves were prepared, but the tenants had refused to pay for them. He also admitted to removing the iron bars in exchange for unpaid rent, but said he later replaced them. We do not know if this dispute ever came to court, but it occurred just before the Civil War at a time of considerable strife between the gentry and the commoner.

Later in 1654, Anthony Smith had enclosed some of the common land on Pudmore Common in an attempt to restrict the peat cutting, which was getting out of control. He issued a writ against the main local families who were travelling from the nearby hamlets of Moushill, Birtley, Wheeler Street, Thursley and from the Hindhead region. The Pudmore region, now called Thursley Common, consisted of 6,000 acres, of which about 50 acres were described as

'bog and quagmire, which could not be walked upon without danger of sinking.'

Anthony Smith argued that stripping the turf adversely affected the pasture and drainage of the area. However, the court found this to be a wrongful reversal of the decision of the Court Baron in 1634, when Henry Bell had opened up the land for peat cutting. Smith then appealed to Oliver Cromwell, who sent a circular to the main 60 tenants of the manor, forbidding them to cut peat on Pudmore Common.

Anthony Smith died on 13 October 1669; he had been Lord of the Manor of Witley for 35 years. His memorial is on the south wall of the Manor Chapel in Witley church. The memorial succinctly describes him as

'Lord of the manor, who was petitioner to King Charles ye 1st and to King Charles ye 2nd.... And to this parish he was an ample benefactor.'

It was in his will, Anthony Smith stated that he wished to be buried in Witley Church, next to his ancestors. He left £80 which was to buy clothes for the oldest poor people in the parishes of Witley and Thursley. The old men were to have black coats and the old women black gowns to keep them warm. He allocated his carp in the hammer ponds of his ironworks between an overseer of the will, his wife and the rest to the freeholder of the ponds.

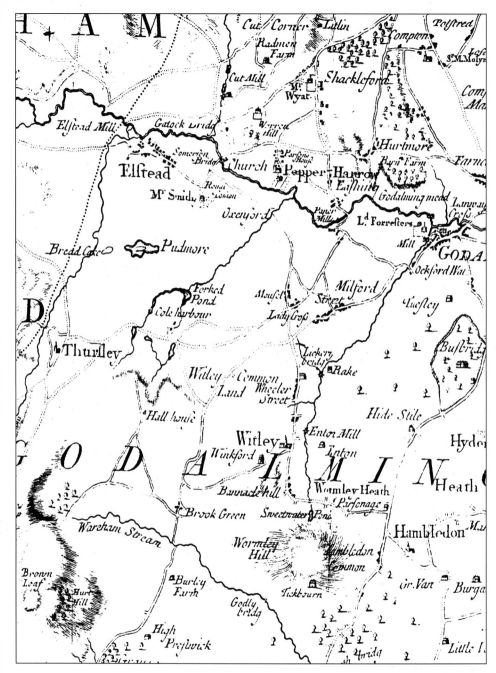

Map of Witley and the surrounding hamlets before the turnpikes.
Drawn by John Senex in 1729. Reproduced courtesy of Harry Margary Maps.

He left generous bequests to the poor children of Witley and Thursley, and £60 for a great tenor bell to be provided in the church - this is still in use today.

The Manor of Witley then passed to Thomas, brother of Anthony Smith, and Rake went to Anthony Smith Meale. It was Thomas Smith's descendants who built Milford House in the early 18th century. Witley Manor passed by marriage to Philip Carteret Webb of Busbridge in 1763. The Carteret Webb memorials can be seen in the Manor Chapel of Witley church.

The 16th and early 17th centuries saw the beginning of settlements outside Witley and Milford. The area around Gurdons in Wormley, *Gordenslond*, was first mentioned in 1500; Brook, *Broke*, or *Broke Strete*, is mentioned in 1548, and Redlands at Sandhills was also mentioned in 1548. Some of this might be due to charcoal production or possibly to early mining operations on the Weald Clays.

By 1729, Brook Green is featured on John Senex's map, but Sandhills does not appear until it is shown as a hamlet on the Rocque map of 1768, with Brook Road shown as Sandell Lane. Bannacle Common is shown and Combe lane at Wormley is named Comb Lane, leading to Comb Common and Comb House. Within the village of Witley, late 16th century development included Church Steps Cottage and Step Cottage, possibly on the site of an earlier dwelling. April Cottage and Cobblers Cottage are dated at about 1600, Old Cottage and Hillbrow as late 16th century. Sun Cottages are about 1600 and By the Way is late 16th century.

The black and white cottages between what was the Sun Inn and Mr Milton's house were held on tenure of the Red Rose Rent. Thomas Stynt, a weaver of Witley, granted a lease of these cottages in 1580 to Richard Paine of Enton for 800 years, for a yearly rent of one red rose. Within two months, he had assigned the lease to John Howick, a butcher of Witley. From then onwards the lease was passed on, until James Pannel, a game-keeper from Elstead, sold the cottage to E. A. Chandler in 1904 and no trace of the red rose freeholder remained.

The period between 1300 and 1700 has been called 'The Little Ice Age' due to the poor climate in Britain, and the period between 1680 and 1703 was one of the coldest in Northern Europe. This coincided with an improvement

The 'Red Rose Cottages' in Witley in 1999.
Reproduced courtesy of Roger Egerton.

in building methods with the that result houses became more substantial. Brick had been introduced towards the end of the Middle Ages and was now widely applied to even simple houses. In the late 16th century and 17th century, glass was increasingly used in the windows of ordinary houses, but it could only be made by hand into small square and diamond-shaped panes.

Water Mills

There was little advance of mill technology from their introduction in Roman times until Saxon times. Benefiting from the plentiful water supply provided by the River Wey, Godalming became a major centre for the manufacture of woollen garments, the principal cottage industry in the area for centuries. Cleaning the natural animal fat from the wool was done with Fuller's Earth, which occurs in vast opencast pits at Redhill.

The earliest suggestion of a mill in the Royal Manor of Witley is in 1321, when Robert de Rake sold two mills at Catteshall, with *'land and appurtenances,'* to Thomas atte Mulle of Catteshall. One was a fulling mill, the other a corn mill. In 1324, Richard de Medemefelde, the son of Robert de Rake, released to Richard le Court of Moushill his right to all lands and tenements and appurtenances in the Parish of Witley. Milford, about a mile to the north, is first mentioned in the Assize Rolls of 1235, as *Muleford*, ford by the mill, and it is very likely but not proven that this refers to Rake Mill.

In 1548, Rake Mill was described as a fulling mill in the Manor of Witley, held by Robert Mellershe with 20 acres of land. This family had lived in the area since the 12th century and the name appears in the area until the 20th century. John Mellershe, son of Robert, had an action brought against him in the Court of the Exchequer between 1576 and 1578, by Thomas Jones. Jones, the son of Henry VIII's food server and taster, was also the King's Steward and Keeper of the Park and in possession of the old rectory manor estates, including Sattenham lying adjacent to Rake Mill. He accused Mellershe of raising the level of the millpond and flooding six or seven acres of good meadow. There is no record of the outcome, but in 1592, the fulling mill and land had passed from Mellershes, the clothiers, to Henry Tanner alias Bell, of Godalming. After the reign of Elizabeth I, the milling soke was gradually relaxed, thus providing the opportunity for new mills to be developed and for modernisation of existing mills, and at this time Henry Bell took the opportunity to rebuild Rake.

In 1676, Rake Mill was operating as a corn mill and was still in operation in 1771, in the possession of the Woods family. In 1836, it passed to Thomas Durrant, a miller from Berkshire, and in 1857 two parcels of land were sold to the Portsmouth Railway Company. The last miller at Rake was Edward Durrant, who died aged 73 in 1898 and was buried at Milford. A full account of the history of Rake is given by Alan Bott in his paper entitled 'Rake Manor, Godalming, Surrey'.

Enton Mill, also on the tiny River Ock, is believed to have been built in the 15th century. In 1604, Thomas Payne owned the watermill and three acres of moor with appurtenances in Godalming and Witley. It will be remembered that Enton was still within the Godalming Hundred until 1905. During the 18th century, Enton Mill was owned by John Chandler, and Thomas Munton was the miller. By 1799, Enton Mill was owned by trustees of John Hall, a papermaker at Eashing Mill. Enton Mill was owned, in 1805, by John Lasham, originally from Brook, then by Richard Snelling until 1838, when it passed to the Whitbourn family, until it closed in 1899. Enton Mill is named on the Senex map of 1729 and again on the Rocque map of 1768.

Enton Mill in 1906, shortly after it closed in 1899 and before conversion into a house. Courtesy of Haslemere Educational Museum.

When it was converted into a house, the millstream was diverted around the west wing and on to the north of the house, where the field was dammed and dredged to form the fishing lake which is now Enton Fisheries. It is believed that the oldest remaining part of the site is the miller's cottage to the east, built in 1621. The ground floor was filled in when the lake was created and only the tops of the windows remain. The present mill was built in 1756, corn being stored on the top floor. It was converted to a house in 1912. The west wing was added in the 1930s.

Cosford Mill near Thursley is also thought to date from the 15th century. In about 1548, Marion Hedger, granddaughter of Thomas Court of Moushill, married Richard Shudd of Cosford. Joan Shudd of Cosford and Moushill married John Stillwell of Lower House, Thursley, and thereby, Cosford Mill passed into the Stillwell family. In 1702, the Stillwells divided the estate, giving Cosford to John and Moushill to his brother Edmund. John Stillwell died in 1767, leaving Cosford to his son James. In 1793, Cosford passed to James' nephew, John Hawkins. The original building of Bargate Stone was extended in brick in 1762. Cosford appears on the Rocque Map of 1768 as 'Thursley Mill'. In 1852, Henry Pope, who owned the Silk Mill, also owned Cosford Mill. He sold the mill to Henry Denyers in 1855, who owned it until 1887.

Tilford Mill was described as a fulling mill in 1367, but by 1679 was a corn mill. It closed in the 1850s.

Thursley Silk Mill was recorded as having two ponds in 1790 and, although shown on the Rocque map in 1768 as an iron mill, was recorded by Thomas Nalder in 1794, as being a silk mill. There were three old cottages here, which would have been built for the ironworkers. In 1849, the silk mill was occupied by Henry Pope, who also owned Cosford Mill. The silk mill had closed by 1871.

Expansion of the milling industry in the first half of the 19th century was linked to the development of the railways, which increased the supply area for buying grain and transporting flour. At this time mills were extended to increase their storage capacity. Many wooden wheels were replaced with cast iron. Construction materials varied across the county depending on the availability of materials. In this locality there was a lack of building stone, so mills were usually constructed from brick and timber. Watermills on the River Wey were characteristic in having a plentiful water supply, so they tended to be larger mills and built of brick. Brick tax was introduced in 1784 and increased again in 1794 and 1803. Therefore weather-boarding became popular. Use of brick increased at the end of the 19th century, after the brick tax was repealed in 1850.

The introduction of steam power, combined with the use of rollers at the end of the 19th century, caused radical change in the milling industry with the eventual decline of the local village water mill. The repeal of the Corn Laws in 1846 allowed vast quantities of foreign wheat to be imported. Large steam mills were set up in and around the port of London. Water-mills on the River Wey navigation (one of the earliest canals to be constructed, navigable to Guildford in 1653 and to Godalming in 1763) were more fortunate than most in being within easy access of the River Thames and were converted to rolling mills. However, our local mills could not compete. Rake Mill was closed in 1895 and Enton Mill in 1899. Eashing Mill had already been converted to papermaking.

The Iron Industry in Witley Park and Surrounding Area

The southern part of the Parish, beyond Wormley, Sandhills and Brook, is mainly Wealden Clay, laid down over 100 million years ago in a vast, stagnant, inland swamp subjected to periodic flooding. Here were the perfect conditions for the formation of bands of ironstone within thick clays and sandstones. Later earth movements and gentle folding produced the area today which we call the Weald Anticline. At the western-most corner of this vast region which stretches from Picardy in North France, through Kent, Sussex, and into Surrey, lies the parish of Witley.

Iron smelting in the Weald is known from at least 300 BC, as a very small-scale production in isolated localities. Sources of iron included the iron-rich sandstones of the Folkestone Beds of the Lower Greensand, found capping Haydon's Ball, and the Commons at Thursley, Hankley and Tilford. Other sources were secondary deposits in gravels and the clay ironstones in the southern region of the parish. Evidence of early iron workings have been found at Hascombe fortified camp and at Pipers Copse and possibly at Burningfold near Dunsfold. Finds of iron cinder and slag of the non-Belgic Iron Age date from about the 7th century BC. This early iron-age was characterised by a non slag-tapping furnace, i.e the ore was crushed and roasted, then put in a large clay crucible and baked at over 1150°C and the molten iron removed. This technique was used in the west, based on techniques from north-west Gaul. Iron production was well established when the Belgic tribes arrived from Europe 200 years later, in the 1st cen-tury BC. The arrival of these tribes brought the introduction of the 'domed slag-tapping furnace'.

When the Romans returned to Britain, during the invasion of AD 43, they noted the main exports from Britain were iron, slaves and dogs. The Romans formalised and developed the industry, particularly in the eastern Weald, where over 36 sites provided large-scale production for export through London and the coastal ports, providing for the needs of the armies and the developing empire into the middle of the 2nd century BC. In the western Weald, the industry continued in the form of small-scale isolated production sites. This free-mining involved prospecting along the small rivers of the Arun drainage basin, and might have included the Wareham Stream to the south of Brook. When the ore was located, vertical shafts were dug, about 2 m in diameter. These pits were later infilled with rubble, to form 'bell pits'. These were called mines, as the local term for ore was 'mine'. Although evidence is sparse, it is possible that free-mining was taking place in our area in Roman times, possibly around the Whitebeech area using the River Arun as a means of transport. Archaeological evidence suggests the villa fell into decline around AD 320. Could it be that some form of industrial activity was resumed by the Anglo-Saxons, requiring slaves mentioned in the Domesday Book? These early bloomeries were very localised and are difficult to identify, particularly as they were often reworked later.

Wealden iron, although high in impurities, continued to be used to provide small armaments such as arrow heads and other small items such as nails, horseshoes and iron bars throughout the Middle Ages. There was a late medieval ironworks at Lurgashall bloomery. The industry was flourishing in the Middle Ages, until hit by repeated epidemics of the Bubonic Plague which swept through the Weald. A particularly bad epidemic in 1360-61 caused the abandonment of many farms. By this time, the woodlands were being managed and coppiced to ensure an adequate supply of fuel for the iron industry. A bloomery required about two acres of wood per year for each ton of iron produced. Trees were cut on a ten or twelve year rotation. In our area, particularly around Chiddingfold, there was considerable competition with the long-established glass-making industry for wood for fuelling furnaces.

Production of iron was intermittent and seasonal. Wood was cut and charcoal produced in winter and early spring. In summer, when the ground had dried out, the ore was mined, roasted and stocks built up ready for smelting in the late summer and autumn. A bloomery might produce 3 or 4 tons per year and one bloom of iron weighed 30 lb. So this relatively small-scale and sustainable activity continued until the revitalisation of the industry in late Tudor times and with the introduction of the blast furnace.

The revival of the Wealden iron industry in Tudor times was fuelled by both the growth of defences of the South Coast and the need to supply the Navy. An influx of French ironworkers who were familiar with the new blast furnaces already being used in Europe helped the industry develop in the Arun basin after 1550. Many older sites were redeveloped due to an Act of Parliament restricting the development of new ironworks and the benefits of reworking the iron-rich cinders. The restriction on development of new ironworks did not apply to the Western Weald, and we therefore have the ironworks at Thursley and Imbhams and West End established at the end of the 16th century and in the early 17th century.

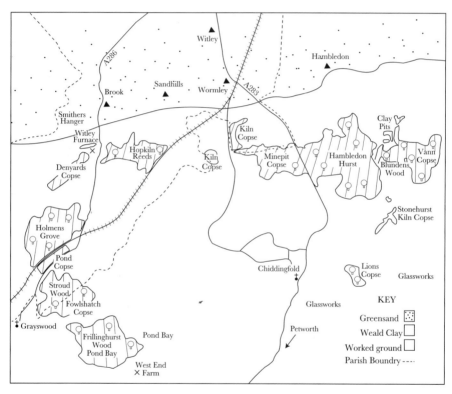

Showing the location of minepits in the southern part of Witley Parish.

At the end of the 16th century, Anthony, Viscount Montague, owned vast areas of land in Sussex and Surrey, including the Waverley Abbey estate which included Oxenford, later sold to Sir George More in 1609. The earliest record of mining in this area is 20th February 1570, when Lord Montague had trouble with commoners at Hambledon Hurst, who resented his woodcutting for the ironworks. Later in 1595, Lord Montague claimed an iron mine at Hambledon and at Minepit Copse near Wormley.

46

It has been estimated that 4,000 acres of coppice were needed to supply a furnace and forge. This could be found from land within a three mile radius, if one quarter of the land were under coppice.

Charcoal production was done locally, and the effects of woodcutting for ironworks in the Eastern Weald was so devastating on the local communities who relied heavily on this natural resource for so many aspects of their daily life, that it prompted an Act of Parliament in 1558, prohibiting the use of wood more than 1ft square at the base. Although the supply of wood was not such a problem in the Western Weald, the Act of Parliament in 1620, requiring only coal to be used in glass manufacture, had a devastating effect on the ancient local glass-working industry based around Chiddingfold.

Ore for the blast furnaces was dug from minepits, the remains of which can be seen in woods and copses and sometimes in fields, extending in a belt from Vann copse near Hambledon, through Blundens Wood, Hambledon Hurst, Minepit Copse, Hopkiln Reeds, Denyards Copse near the blast furnace at Wareham House, then on to Holmens Grove, Pond Copse, and Stroud Wood, to the parish boundary. Minepits continue through Fowlspatch Copse to Frillinghurst Wood, where there was a blast furnace at West End, then on to Imbham's Furnace.

This area formed a distinct iron-ore field serving a group of furnaces. Evidence of mining in this area was preserved in the names of fields which appear on the 1844 Tithe map, such as Little Minepits and Great Minepits at Wareham Farm.

The ironworks at Thursley were not listed in the inventory of Wealden ironworks in 1574, but were first mentioned in a lease of 14th May 1610, and were amongst the last to be set up in Surrey. Sir Robert More established the works early in the 1600s, then leased them in 1610 to Sir Edward More for a rent of £95 per year and in exchange for delivery of that most vital fuel source, wood.

Map showing the site of the iron works on Thursley and Witley Commons in 1768. From Rocque's Map. Reproduced courtesy of Harry Margary Maps.

In 1931, the industrial archaeologist, Earnest Straker, found three forge sites at Upper Hammer and Lower Hammer on a westerly stream flowing from Cosford through the ironworks and into Forked Pond. The third forge, Coldharbour Hammer (Horsebane Hammer), was sited on the easterlystream partly in Witley, partly in Thursley. A deed of 1617, drawn up at the time Henry Bell leased the ironworks from the Moores, lists hammers, bellows, hammer beams and implements along with workmen's houses recently built on the heath. There were ponds, water courses and bays for storage of coals (charcoal), iron sows and cinders.

In March 1623, the Mores sold the ironworks for £200 to Henry Bell, described as 'now of Milford', so it is assumed he had moved from Godalming to his recently rebuilt house at Rake.

On 1st April 1634, that is a few weeks before his death, Henry Bell passed the ironworks over to his great nephew, Anthony Smith of Witley. Smith leased the works to Francis Wyatt for seven years at £40 per year. It was then described as

> 'a forge or ironwork called Horsebane Hammer and one furnace and ironworks newly erected near the forge all situated in Witley and Thursley heaths.'

Horsebane Hammer lay one mile to the North East of Thursley church. The Rocque map of 1768 shows the A3 London to Portsmouth road running between two large ponds with an awkward bend. The road was later straightened and taken to the east across another pond which does not exist now. The Lower Hammer ironworks was converted to a silk mill, 'Crape mill', by 1805, but traces of 17th century masonry, slag and carrstone remain.

In 1666, on 1st June, the ironworks were leased for two years to William Yalden the elder, an ironmaster of considerable repute from Blackdown in Sussex. The Yaldens settled in the area around Thursley and Haslemere. Yalden leased the ironworks for only £10 per year, compared with the rent of £95 in 1610 and £40 in 1634. However, the upper finery was excluded from the lease and Yalden was charged with paying local taxes to the church and for the poor. The chimney tax, or Hearth Tax, had also just been introduced. If Anthony Smith wished to fish from the Forked Pond which lay below the Hammer Pond, he was to advise Yalden so that he could stop the water from the higher pond flowing into Forked Pond and thereby disturbing the fish. Regarding fuel for the ironworks, Anthony Smith was now providing 200 cords of wood from within the parish of Witley at the rate of five shillings a cord to be provided in May and paid for on the 1st November. (A cord of wood was a parcel of firewood.) Anthony Smith was therefore receiving fifty pounds per year for firewood, which was considerably more than the rent of the ironworks. The wood was to be turned into charcoal or 'coaled' in the nearby coppices owned by Anthony Smith, and Yalden had the right to make pits and move earth as necessary for making charcoal.

In the eighteenth century, the iron forges were still used for pig iron bars carried from the barges on the Wey Navigation in Godalming, using the newly constructed turnpike road. Although the Wey Navigation was built as far as Guildford in 1653, it was not until 110 years later that it was extended to the Warf in Godalming. The main trade between the Weald and London was in timber, cut planks, hoops, bark, flour and iron goods. This trade had previously used the turnpiked roads, passing through the toll-gate at Meadrow in Godalming. When the Wey Navigation opened, this trade was made to pass direct to the Warf and avoiding the toll-gate. A proposal in 1767 to move the toll-gate between Guildford and Godalming was made because, the traffic to and from the ironworks between Milford and Hindhead now used the Kingston to Sheetbridge toll-road without passing through a toll-gate, and therefore did not contribute anything towards the support of the road.

It was agreed that the toll-gate should be moved to the south of Godalming near Ockford Mill. By 1790, the ironworks had closed. The relocated turnpike was demolished when the railway was built in 1856. A third turnpike was built but only operated until 1870.

Turnpike Through Milford and Witley

One of the first and most important changes which affected the way of life for many living in the rural areas, particularly the more wealthy, was the laying down of the turnpike roads. It is amazing that since the building of roads by the Romans, very little repair or replacement had been undertaken until the mid-18th century. In 1531, the Statute of Bridges empowered Justices of the Peace to impose local taxes for the repair and maintenance of broken bridges. By 1555 highways had become *very noisesome and tedious to travel in and dangerous for all passengers and carriages*, so the responsibility for upkeep of roads was transferred to parishes through the first Statute of Highways. Two unpaid Highway Surveyors were elected to make reports on the state of the roads and to supervise the statutory four day's work on the roads each year. Later the number of statutory days for repair work was increased to six days, or to provide two men and a cart for two days. Gravel and other materials could be taken for the repair of roads without asking permission.

By 1700, it was generally accepted that most roads in the area were impassable to wheeled traffic for four or five months of the year. Roads varied from dustbowls in summer to quagmires in winter with four-foot deep ruts and potholes, which would fill with water after rain. Rudimentary repairs involved filling in ruts and holes with bundles of wood. The greatest users of the roads were therefore people on foot and animals.

In 1703, Prince George of Denmark, husband of Queen Anne, travelled from Windsor to Petworth. The journey took 14 hours, with only nine miles being covered in the last six hours. One of the worst spots was around Hambledon, where the Royal coach had to be manhandled out of the clay and several accompanying coaches were overturned. The Prince recorded in his diary that the roads were *'the worst ways ever seen'*.

Before the days of the Turnpike Trusts, signposting of ways was very poor and the twistiness of some of the roads meant that travellers frequently lost their way. In the reign of Charles II, Samuel Pepys lost his way at Hindhead and in 1820, William Cobbett described the same locality as *'the most villainous spot God ever made'*. Highwaymen were a constant hazard to travellers, and in 1720 in one week, all the coaches running from London to Surrey were attacked and robbed. Hindhead was a notorious blackspot.

Map showing the new turnpike over Wormley Hill, from Rocque's map of 1768.
Reproduced courtesy of Harry Margary Publications Ltd.

Wormley Hill was another bad spot when the turnpike road across it was opened in 1750. This was a deserted place and heavily wooded, providing excellent cover for highwaymen. There were no houses nearby until the Fox and Hounds public house was built in 1800. This provided a place of refreshment for travellers, and it became a favourite meeting place for workers on the Witley Park estate and later, the builders of King Edward's School and new houses in Wormley and along Brook Road. The site is now marked by the Fox and Hounds Cottages belonging to King Edward's School.

Bad weather was another hazard and even in the days of the Turnpike, passengers travelling on the top of the coach had been known to die of exposure during the journey. At Hindhead in 1836, a great traffic jam was recorded in deep snow, with many coaches stranded at Thursley. The Royal mails were taken off to safety by the devoted guards and the only coach to get through was the Star of Brunswick driven by a local man.

River crossings were another hazard. Even in Godalming until 1782, there was no public bridge over the River Wey. The only bridge belonged to the Loseley Manor and it was open to the public only in times of flood.

In 1681, there was a daily coach from London to Portsmouth through Godalming and Milford. In 1749, one of the first turnpikes to be built in the country was the Godalming to Hindhead road. The road was lowered by 60ft near the Devil's Punchbowl in 1826, to make the climb to Hindhead less difficult for the horses. Many eminent sailors such as Drake and Nelson travelled on this road, using the coaching inns at Guildford, Godalming and Hindhead.

After the road over Wormley Hill was opened in 1750, the coach to Petworth departed from Great Lombard Street in London. Fares on the outside seats cost 3d per mile, inside seats cost 5d per mile. Horses, Cleveland Bays, were changed about every 15 miles allowing three minutes for the change.

In the 19th century one of the main coaches running over Wormley Hill was the 'Earl of March', from Witley to Chiddingfold, Petworth and Midhurst. This was a Chilman's coach, painted yellow with details in black. After 1859, a coach ran from Witley railway station to Chichester.

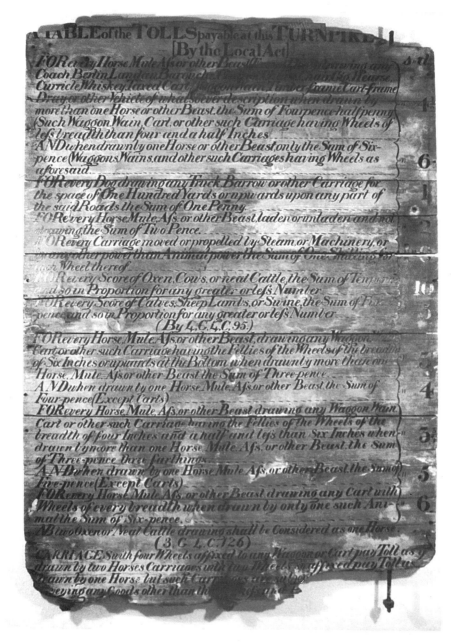

Photograph of the Tolls on the Toll board from the Turnpike between Wormley and Chiddingfold. Reproduced courtesy of Haslemere Educational Museum.

Stocking knitting frame of the type used in Witley and Milford in the 17th century. Reproduced courtesy of Godalming Museum.

The Clothing Industry in Witley and Milford

The traditional woollen industry based on the short-stapled fleece, and using local fulling mills, was declining towards the end of the 17th century because of the introduction of the long-staple fleece and the resulting change from demand for woollens to worsteds. Clothing families moved into the framework knitting industry, making stockings. Some of these came from 17th century blacksmith families, such as the Tickners. Henry Sad was a silk weaver in Milford in 1676, and Richard Chitty and Caleb Tickner were framework knitters in 1696. Framework knitters were first recorded in Godalming in 1681, but by the late 17th century, framework knitting had replaced cloth manufacture as the textile industry of South West Surrey.

The industry was dispersed amongst the towns and villages and, with Godalming as a major centre, the villages of Eashing, Milford, Thursley, Witley, Hambledon, Chiddingfold and Haslemere all had framework knitters. In the 18th century, Witley had as many as six apprentices to the industry.

Local family names associated with the framework knitting industry were Bowler, Chitty, Hooke, Monger, Parkhurst, Shrubb, Toft and Woods.

At the turn of the century, William Boys was vicar of the parish of Witley from 1699 to 1735, and the population was 1000. There were about 12 marriages each year, 20 births and 16 burials. The climate was improving and summers were glorious.

Chapter 4

Changing Society from 1800 to 2000

Social Developments in Witley and Milford

In the early 1800s, Milford was described by Manning and Bray as 'an airy and pleasant village', and Moushill was a small hamlet containing Oxenford, Borough, Sattenham and Rake. Oxenford Grange had been a Nunnery built near a well, which was reputed for its healing powers, particularly for eyes and ulcers. The Grange was demolished in 1775 and the masonry used in the construction of the mansion at Peper Harow Park. Pugin was employed by the 5th Viscount Middleton to build an imitation 13th century farm there, which can still be seen today. By 1844, Viscount Middleton owned many farms around Oxenford, including Bagmoor, Misslebrook, Rices, Thurnets Wood and Great Kennel Moor. The Tithe Map of 1844 records Dog Kennels here, and this could have been the home of the Milford, Godalming and District Harriers established sometime before 1897. This pack of foot beagles, known as the Horsell, is recorded in the Victoria County History.

By 1801, the population of Witley was 1,039, little changed compared with the previous century, and living conditions were poor. Deteriorating climate in the early part of the 19th century affected harvests and the cost of food rose sharply. The following years brought a general economic slow down, social upheaval and disease. Outbreaks of disease were frequent and the infant death rate was high, so that births each year were almost matched by the number of burials in Witley and Milford. Throughout the countryside the need to support the Napoleonic Wars, and the rising unemployment when they ended, together with the failure of harvests in 1810 and 1811, hit the rural people hard. These depravations did not deter the clergy from reforming the local landscape. Sometime between 1763 and 1809, Rev. John Flutter Chandler modernised the 16th century Vine House, now called The Manor, and created ponds on five acres of boggy ground along the River Ock. During the following decades, he and his son Rev. John Chandler entertained friends on fishing expeditions when pike of up to 33 lbs weight were recorded.

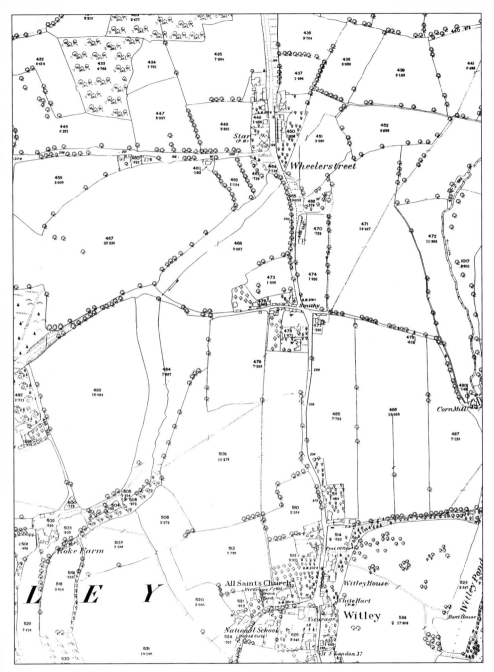

Extract from the 1:25,000 scale Ordnance Survey map of 1870, showing Wheeler Street. Reproduced by permission of Surrey History Service.

As long ago as 1572 an Act of Parliament had allowed parishes to provide for their own poor people. This law was refined in 1596 to identify 'the deserving poor' and parishes either provided food and clothing or housed them in a workhouse. The provision for the poor, until the reform of the Poor Law in 1834, remained the responsibility of the parish. Overseers for the parish collected the poor rate and arranged the distribution of relief.

In 1834, there were just 169 houses in Witley and a population of about 1,400. It is not surprising that 458 of the occupants of Witley and Milford were receiving poor relief in the early 19th century. At this time, 60% of the population were under the age of 30 and mostly without employment. The main employment for males was, not surprisingly, as agricultural labourers. Young males between the ages of 10 and 19 were often employed as male servants in the large houses such as Milford House and later at Witley Park. Girls were most often employed as female servants until they reached their late twenties or became married, after which time they were classified as 'unemployed'!

Witley, unlike the majority of parishes, could be considered fortunate in that it could afford to house its own poor. The paupers with no home of their own were lodged in the House of Industry, which is now a row of cottages at the end of Wheeler Lane, opposite the Star public house. The Master's, or Guardian's, house was the larger building at the north end of the row, where in the early 19th century, William Richardson supplemented his income with framework knitting.

The poor were put to work either in the House itself or in the four acre Workhouse Meadow behind the House of Industry, or on the parish land on Milford Heath, which was later enclosed and lies in the vicinity of the cemetery. In 1826, it was decided that the inhabitants should be well fed and clothed and that a skilled surgeon-apothecary should be employed to look after their general health. Conditions here appear to have been reasonably comfortable and it must have been a difficult decision to re-locate to Hambledon.

Many parishes throughout the country could not afford to look after their rising numbers of destitute inhabitants, both agricultural workers and men returning from the wars, often wounded and unable to work, so the Gilbert Act of 1782 allowed parishes to unite to run a jointly operated workhouse.

The workhouse for the Hambledon Union was built on the southern edge of Wormley Hill in 1786. In 1831, the Hambledon Union Workhouse had nine member parishes (Bramley, Chiddingfold, Dunsfold, Hambledon, Hascombe, Haslemere, St. Martha's, Shalford and Wonersh) and eighty eight inhabitants.

After 1834, when the Poor Law effectively forced parishes to join the Union by removing control from local parishes and transfer responsibility to a regional Board of Guardians, it must have been increasingly difficult for parishes such as Witley and Thursley to continue their provision. When Witley's House of Industry was eventually closed down in 1836 and purchased by the Board of Governors for the Hambledon Union in 1840 for the handsome price of £2,287.7s.0d. the Hambledon building was enlarged to accommodate the poor from seven new parishes including Witley, Thursley, Peper Harow and Elstead, in addition to the nine original member parishes. Conditions here must have been much less comfortable with the abolition of provision for outdoor work. The food was poor, and a general philosophy aimed at encouraging the inmates to seek employment elsewhere as soon as possible made conditions for the occupants less than convivial.

The bulk of the tithe-producing land was nearly 3,000 acres of arable land, growing mainly oats (517 bushels), then barley (360 bushels) and wheat (203 bushels). There were only 800 acres of meadow and pasture.

The 20 farmers provided employment for 180 agricultural workers from the Witley and Milford area, including 126 acres at Roake, which was farmed by Thomas Stovold in 1868. C. Lickfold occupied Winkford Farm and John White was a farmer from Brook. John Sparkes at Chisbury was also farming land at Bannacle, Colmoor and Ladds on the northern slope of Wormley Hill as well as cutting peat from the moor to the north east of Borough Farm, where Thomas Mansell farmed.

A gathering of local Witley folk outside the 'White Hart' about 1883.
Reproduced courtesy of Haslemere Educational Museum.

There were two gamekeepers, a miller at Rake, a papermaker, a miller and farmer called T. Whitbourn at Enton, and a relative, Arthur Whitbourn, was a maltster at malthouse cottages, built at the end of a lane now leading to Enton Fisheries with the Malthouse Meadow behind. The Whitbourns lived at Parsonage Farm and leased land at Wheeler Street and Crossways. The map by John Senex, published in 1729, shows a few cottages at Crossways, and in 1844 Thomas Young had a shop and garden on the site where the newsagents shop of T. E. Francis now stands. By 1870 there was a Smithy here.

There were plenty of public houses in the area and Jacob Smithers beer house to be supplied. In Milford, the White Lion public house was owned by William Elkins and run by John Gosling. The Red Lion public house was run by Edward Mandeville. In Witley, the White Hart was run by Harriet White, and the Sun Inn, where the Sun Cottage now stands, was run by Mr. Yelding in 1868. The Wood Pidgeon run by Mrs. Over, catered for the needs of the rail passengers at the newly built 'Witley for Chiddingfold' station. J. Rollet ran the Fox and Hounds on Wormley Hill and further along the road to Chiddingfold, James Puttock ran The Wheatsheaf. The tiny hamlet of Brook also had its own maltster, James Heward, at the malt house supplying the Dog and Pheasant, and Mr. Welland ran the village shop and Post Office from Sister Cottage. The tithe map of 1844 shows a blacksmith on the corner of the little lane, which now leads to the Pirrie Hall, but there is no sign of its existence today. There was also an alehouse called Sebastopol in Sandhills, which is now April Cottage.

The villages and hamlets at this time were endowed with more shops than we have today; even Brook had a shop. In Witley there was a cordwainer's run by Peter Howard on Lashams Hill. (A cordwainer was a shoemaker who used the type of Spanish leather from Cordova in Spain.) A pond existed a little to the north of where the War Memorial now stands and the Rev. John Chandler occupied Vine House next to The White Hart. The school was no more than a cottage opposite an old barn on the corner in Church Lane in 1844, before adjoining land was used in the rebuild of 1898. Mr. R. Bridger was the parish schoolmaster for 30 years. As well as the shop at Crossways, there was a shop owned by William Bridger opposite the House of Industry, next to where the Star is now.

View from the end of Church Lane, Witley, showing the joiner's shop, which was moved to the Weald and Downland Museum. Photographed in October 1883. Reproduced courtesy of Haslemere Educational Museum.

In Milford, William Young was a nurseryman, on land roughly where Secretts Farm now lies. There were two shops on the Portsmouth Road, but the main settlement was along Church Road, where Richard Burdock and Charles Bowler both had shops. There were eight shoemakers and a tanner. One surgeon, three teachers, a telegraph assistant and a letter boy are included amongst the local inhabitants at the time. New forms of employment were emerging; for example, George Edwards operated the Turnpike on the Haslemere Road at Stroud Gate.

At the time of the 1841 census, there were in Witley three blacksmiths, three brickburners and six bricklayers, one builder, 11 carpenters and 11 sawyers, suggesting a thriving construction industry.

Brick and tile making was an important industry at this time, probably due to the lack of building stone in the area, and the Atherfield Clay being a preferred source to the Weald Clay. An extensive brickworks is shown on the 1844 Tithe Map at Wareham, Brook. The site occupying more than ten acres was owned by Miltons of Witley. In Kelly's Directory of Surrey, 1895, Frank Milton was described as a 'builder, contractor, undertaker, decorator and plumber; estimates given for general repairs'. Miltons brickworks which supplied the building materials was run by a Mr. C. Mercer in 1937. He was 78 and had worked there for over 50 years. Brickburning took place once a fortnight and one man could produce over 1,000 bricks per day and 900 tiles. Five men were employed and they worked in the copses during the winter months. There was a small brick works in Park Copse opposite Halnacker. Another major brickworks in the area was owned by Messrs. Cooper of Combe Lane, Witley, who also owned the walking stick factory, which was supplied by the extensive chestnut coppices in the Wormley area. Their brick works in Chiddingfold had been in use since before 1835 and employed as many as 25 men in 1937. A smaller works at Cuckoo Corner was set up in 1935, but this appears to have been little used and had a low production in 1937.

In 1851, before the railway arrived, the population recorded in the census was only 1,546. However by 1871, ten years after the railway was opened, the population had increased to 1,764 and has risen steadily since then. Mr Edward Dibben was the Postmaster and kept the local stores. The Post Office was on Lashams Hill and the letters arrived every day at 7.40 a.m. and left at 5.55 p.m., and at 10.45 a.m. on Sundays.

There was a leap in population in the 1880s and 1890s, when many artistic folk left London to escape the various epidemics, which were sweeping the city, for the supposedly improved climate of Wormley and Sandhills. By 1901, the census shows a population of 2,827.

Historically combined within Witley, Thursley took its first moves towards independence when it started its own Parish Register in 1559, and was considered to be a separate parish by 1804. From about the 1730s to 1833,

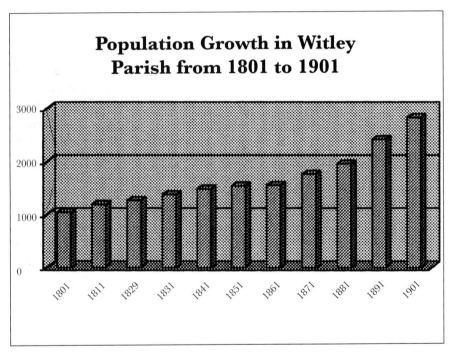

Population growth in Witley and Milford.

there were voluntary groupings of parishes for Poor Law purposes. However, when the House of Industry in Witley closed in 1834 and Witley and Thursley both joined the Hambledon Union, the decision was made to form a separate ecclesiastical parish of Thursley.

The church of St John, Milford, was built in 1837, as part of a regional church-building scheme of the Bishop of Winchester. The Rev. John Flutter Chandler, Vicar of Witley and also the Rural Dean, performed the consecration service of the new church on 31st January, 1837. He was an elderly man of 75 years and perhaps it was due to the occasion or the winter climate, but he died that same evening. It was not until 1844, that the diocese could afford to provide for Milford as a separate Parish. Until that time, the Rev. John Chandler (1806-1876) would spend his time between Witley, Thursley and Milford churches. The Local Government Act of 1894 gave democratic control to parish councils, and the two par-ishes of Milford and Witley shared a common Parish Council then, as they do today.

At the entrance to the lane from Milford Heath to Wheeler Street was a small stream running through a tunnel under the Petworth turnpike road, shown on John Senex's map dated 1729, as Lickery Bridge. This feeder stream to the River Ock runs under the Petworth Road alongside the entrance to Rodborough School. Another feeder stream is shown on the Rocque Map of 1768 running from Rock Farm and is now piped underground beneath the Willow Mead housing development to the pond, now drained and filled in, at Dittons Corner outside the entrance to Chiburys.

In 1876, there was a cholera epidemic then a typhus epidemic. The summer of 1879 saw average temperatures of only 13.7°C with twice the normal rainfall, which cut the wheat harvest by half. Agriculture was in decline and to meet demand, the UK allowed massive imports of grain from North America, and this was a major factor in the demise of our local corn mills. From this period onwards, the increased mechanization of agricultural practice, and the improved transport network of road and rail, ensured that the function and nature of the hamlets and villages was transformed for ever.

The pond and stream at Dittons Corner, Wheeler Street, before it was filled in and grassed over sometime before 1923, as the road here was considered to be treacherous. Reproduced courtesy of John Young.

Semaphore at Bannacle Hill

In 1803, Admiral Sir Home Popham produced a two-arm semaphore system capable of passing a message between the Admiralty and Plymouth in three minutes. Some telegraph stations were converted to semaphore. Stations for the new line to Portsmouth were constructed in 1821/22, and the line operated between 1822 and 1847, providing a reliable means of communication until replaced by the electric telegraph in 1848.

The semaphore on Bannacle Hill at Sandhills was so regular that it provided regular time checks for the locals. Communication was with the Royal Navy and with the Revenue branch in its anti-smuggling activities.

The stations were built to a standard design of brick with brown stucco and varied in height depending on their location. The station at Bannacle Hill was the highest station between the Admiralty and Portsmouth, having four stories with a 30 ft tall hollow hexagonal timber mast. Two arms 8 ft by

16 ins, one set 12 ft above the base and the other at the top of the mast, were painted red for easier identification of the signals. The machinery consisted of two winch handles and a series of ropes and pulleys which could register 48 separate shutter movements.

Staffed by a naval officer with an assistant, the stations were manned night and day. The naval officers were often Lieutenants with no promotion prospects and the assistants would usually be wounded pensioners. The operators worked from the inside of the building. In some cases, especially for sending signals to ships, the mast could be rotated through a full circle.

The first record of a resident officer at Bannacle Hill was Lt. Garrett, when in 1829, he recorded the baptism of a child in Witley Parish church. In 1832, Lt. O'Callaghan also recorded a baptism. Signalman Blurton recorded the burial of a child of only six months old in 1841.

The salary of a Lieutenant was, in 1823, £182.10.0 per year, and the assistants received 2/- per day.

The last semaphore message was transmitted on 31st December 1847 by Signalman Osborne, the last operator, and later, the station at Bannacle Hill was demolished and the land de-requisitioned. Only hollows in the ground remain in the site, which is set back slightly from the Church Lane road in the grounds of Woodbury.

The Arrival of the Railway

In 1803, William Jessop conducted a survey, probably for a tramway. An experienced railway engineer, he had already built several lines and had been responsible for moving the guiding flange from the rail to the wheel. At this time, the estimated cost for the London-Portsmouth line was £400,000, compared with £800,000 for a canal system. By 1845, the South Western Railway had reached Guildford, and it reached Godalming in 1849, terminating at the old station just south of Farncombe. The opening of the line was delayed until October 1849, due to the collapse of the sand tunnel outside Guildford. Before the Witley route was constructed, trains from London to Portsmouth ran via Nine Elms, Vauxhall, Bishopstoke, Eastleigh, north of Southampton, then eastwards to Gosport, then to Harbour Ferry and Portsmouth. The proposed direct route was

74.5 miles long, and there was considerable competition between London and South Western Railway (LSWR), London, Brighton and South Coast Company (LBSC) and the South Eastern and Chatham Railway (SECR).

In July 1853, the Direct Portsmouth Line Act of Parliament was passed, allowing the Havant to Godalming section of 32 miles via Petersfield, Haslemere and Witley to be constructed with capital of £400,000.

The two-year contract of £350,000 was awarded to Thomas Brassey to sell or rent at the end. In August 1853, the first turf was cut. The engineer was Joseph Locke who had worked for many years with the famous Stephenson family of railway engineers, and had designed the 'bull head' rail with a thickened top to take heavier locomotives and allow greater speeds. The gradient of 1 in 80 after Witley presented problems, as did the need for cuttings and embankments. An emergency engine was kept at Haslemere for use in the busy holiday period.

Milford Station in the age of steam. Reproduced courtesy of John Young.

After nearly five years, work was completed on the single-track line. The Haslemere, Witley and Liss cuttings occupied the last two years, with 1,000 men and up to 250 horses employed. Initially, long delays were caused by hostility from the rival LBSC Company, running trains from Havant to Portsmouth. The issue was forced on 28th December 1858, when LSWR sent a goods train to Havant to go on to the Portsmouth terminal. The train carried 100 platelayers and reached Havant at 7 a.m., three hours early. However, the LBSC had removed the points and placed an engine to block the line. The LSWR replaced the points and seized the LBSC engine, but later retreated when a rival army removed a rail from the main line.

On 1st January 1859, the line was opened, but with a horse-drawn bus link from Havant to Portsmouth until the argument with LBSC was resolved. Following a fare war, at great cost to both companies, a legal settlement involving profit sharing was reached.

The Milford and Witley stations were opened on 1st January 1859, and the stationmaster at Witley was Mr. J. Brown. (The Witley station, in neo-Georgian brick with slate roof, remains much the same today, but the up platform has been modified for faster and longer trains.) At this time, the new station was opened at Godalming, although the old one remained in use until 1897 when it was replaced by Farncombe station.

By 1865, the LSWR service on the line was not good, with only four passenger and one goods train each way on weekdays, and no train on Sundays and no express train. By 1868, there were five trains daily each way. The fairs to Godalming from Witley were:

3rd class.....4d. single,.....7d return. 1st class..... 9d. single,.....1s.2d return.

A Witley to Waterloo cheap day return in 1880 cost 7s.6d. 1st class and 5s.6d. 2nd class. The LSWR livery was light green, lined in chocolate brown, black and white for passenger locomotives; the carriages were brown with salmon pink upper panels and the wagons were in dark brown.

By 1st March 1878, the line was doubled all the way through after the line had made a profit of £45,000 in one year. In 1904, a wooden footbridge was built over the line at Witley station for safety reasons.

In 1921, the Railways Act grouped the railways into four mainline comp-anies; the London to Portsmouth Line came under Southern Railway. The line was electrified in 1937 after three million passengers had been carried in that year. The total volume of passengers in 1947 had risen to over seven and a half million. The railways were nationalized in 1948, when Milford and Witley came under the Southern Region.

'Witley for Chiddingfold Station' soon after the footbridge was erected.
Courtesy of John Young.

Schools

To reflect social change and demands of an increasing population in the 19th century, National Schools were built in the villages. This formalised the education of young children, replacing the somewhat sporadic previous arrangements. The first National School was built by John Flutter Chandler in 1834 in Church Road, on the site of the present infant school. There were 211 pupils, and the increasing local population required the school to be extended in 1881 and then rebuilt in 1898.

Grayswood National School was built in 1864, through the generosity of Rev. John Chandler of Witley. It had 81 scholars and was enlarged in 1883.

Milford Church of England School was built in 1850. It had 336 pupils and was enlarged in 1890. Brook Infant School was built in 1882 by means of a donation from Mrs. J. Foster, wife of the philanthropist and brother of Birket Foster, who lived at The Mount in Witley.

At about this time, King Edward's School moved from Southwark to its present site on Wormley Hill in 1867. This site was considered to be perfect, providing plenty of space and clean air for the children, and owing to the new rail link to London for communications with the City of London. So, in 1867, one hundred boys moved to Witley. Although the Charitable Foundation retained its responsibility to the girls' education, it was not until 1952 that they joined the boys at Witley.

Residents from Wormley and Sandhills, many of whom had moved out of London, became involved with the school and usually attended the chapel for Sunday worship. Sir Arthur Conan Doyle was reported to have worshipped at the chapel.

Many of the boys left school to enlist in the Royal Navy or the Army, and in 1870, naval uniform was adopted, a uniform which was to survive for 80 years. In addition to classroom subjects, the boys were taught trades and were seconded to various school departments. The school was, thereby, virtually self-supporting. Discipline was harsh in those days. Drills, parades and inspections were the norm and holidays were not usual. The boys slept in hammocks. The curriculum was very narrow. Three days each week were spent in the classroom and the other three in workshops, e.g. tailor's or boot making.

Music featured prominently in the daily routine of 40 or 50 boys. Edward Rudge, the Chaplain-Superintendent for 30 years, appointed a bandmaster and the school's military band became renowned over a wide area. Many boys went on to take up positions in leading orchestras. Myles Birket Foster, son of the celebrated watercolour painter, was a fellow of the Royal Academy of Music and the family took part in annual concerts at the school, to which many local people were invited. The military band was in great demand in the Witley and Milford area, its inspiring music leading Empire Day Parades, Jubilees and Fetes.

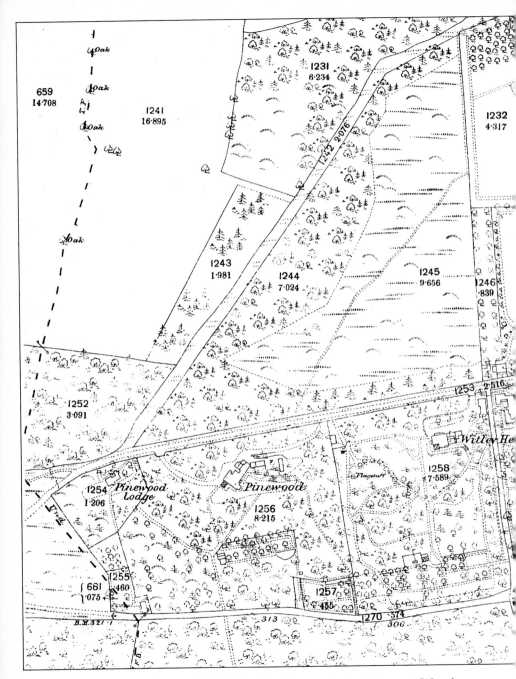

The Ordnance Survey map of 1870 showing the new school and houses at Wormley.
Reproduced courtesy of Surrey History Service.

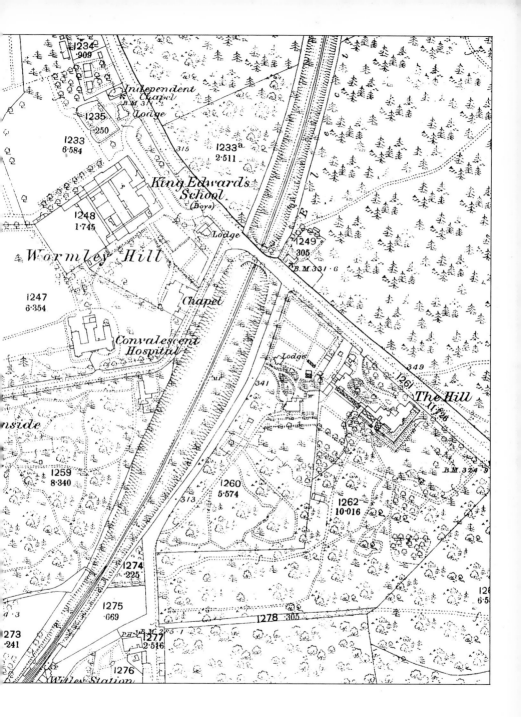

Artistic Inspirations in Witley, Wormley and Sandhills

In 1862, Myles Birket Foster spent a holiday in Witley with his five young children and decided to stay. Living first at Tigbourne Cottage in New Road at the bottom of Wormley Hill, he later bought a large piece of land, about 20 acres, on Wormley Hill, on which he built a mock Tudor house which he called The Hill. Birket Foster moved to The Hill in 1884. The roof was made of old tiles salvaged from local derelict cottages, and stained glass window panes were inscribed with musical scores on the advice of his close friend Charles Keene. William Morris designed the interior and Sir Edward Burne-Jones painted the frieze in the dining room and designed tiles for the fireplaces. Birket Foster died in 1899 and is buried in Witley churchyard.

The Hill, home of Birket Foster, photographed in 1932 when it was sold.
Reproduced courtesy of John Young.

Birket Foster and Alfred Cooper painted the sign for the White Hart, which is now in the Victoria and Albert Museum in London. Birket Foster's son, William Foster, was also an accomplished water-colour artist.

Edmund Evans, the successful colour printer of children's books, which were illustrated by people such as Kate Greenway, Randolph Caldicott and Walter Crane, was a very close friend of Birket Foster. On his marriage, Birket Foster gave his lifelong friend a plot of land next to his own as a wedding present, on which Evans built Leybourne in Combe Lane.

Birket Foster's brother, John, also moved to Witley and built a house, Fernside, on the Brook Road. John Foster was a considerable benefactor to Witley, paying £2,000 for the construction of the Witley Men's Institute, now the British Legion, in 1883. Mrs. John Foster gave money for the construction of Brook Infant School in 1882. It was through his connections with John Foster, that Sir Aston Webb was commissioned to decorate the chancel of Witley Church in 1889, based on symbolism of the communion of the saints. John Foster died at the turn of the century and was buried in Witley churchyard.

By 1870, Witley was increasingly popular with artistic people. The unspoilt landscape, uninterrupted views and picturesque cottages were inspirational. William and Helen Allingham moved to Sandhills hamlet with two small children in 1881. Helen, an artist of immense talent, often accompanied Lord Tennyson, who lived in Haslemere, on his walks, and noticing the rapidly changing nature of the countryside, she decided to record the rural scenes. As a result, we have many idyllic scenes of rural life including cottages in Witley, Sandhills, Hambledon and Godalming, some of which no longer survive. In the summer of 1884, she painted the old cottages in the centre of Witley on the Petworth Road. These cottages were pulled down in 1885 and at the time, the workmen observed they were difficult to dismantle due to the *'sound, firm old oaken beams.'* They must have been regarded with some considerable affection locally, as the water colour artist Birket Foster wanted to relocate them in the extensive grounds of The Hill between Combe Lane and New Road, Wormley.

George Eliot bought The Heights on Brook Road for £5,000 and described it as her *'modest little refuge in the not too distant country'*. Whilst living there, she wrote her last novel, Daniel Deronda. Further along Brook Road, at Pinewood, lived John Clarke Hook R.A., an accomplished marine painter. He was a friend of the Palmer family, famous Surrey landscape painters and engravers from Redhill. Whilst staying at Wormley, H. Sutton Palmer painted many local scenes including Milford Heath, Sandhills, Roake

The old cottages in the centre of Witley, photographed in March 1885.
Reproduced courtesy of Haslemere Educational Museum.

The replacement cottages designed by Penfold and built by October 1885.
Reproduced courtesy of Haslemere Educational Museum.

Farm and Royal Common, to illustrate the book on Surrey by A. J. Moncrieff. Hook did not stay long in Wormley, preferring to move to Churt in 1866, when *'the construction of a huge, hideous brick box to be crammed with hapless children'* threatened his sense of well-being.

W. Graham Robertson, painter, illustrator and playwright, bought Sandhills, recently renamed Sandhills House, on Brook Road from William and Helen Allingham for £5,000 in 1888. There he set up a studio in a barn, where he designed and painted theatre sets. The actress Ellen Terry was a frequent visitor. He wrote pageants and plays and formed a group called the Chiddingfold Players. During the early 1900s, Robertson acquired a large area of land and most of the cottages in Sandhills, including Redlands and Sandhills Common. He donated the Common to the National Trust for safe-keeping in 1935, and on his death he left many of the cottages to their occupiers. The small plot of recreation ground between Sandhills and Hatch Lane is called Robertson's Green, in recognition of his generosity in the area. Robertson originally left the land as a gift from him to the local people to be used for allotments, which remained in use until 1994.

A significant influence on the architecture of substantial properties in West Surrey was Sir Edwin Lutyens. Born in London in 1869, he spent his childhood at Thursley where he was influenced by the use of stone, brick and timber and where he met Gertrude Jekyll. Although he did not live here, Lutyens designed many houses in the area, including two in Church Road, Milford, and Tigbourne Court at the bottom of Wormley Hill. Lutyens' architectural style is still copied today in various aspects of the design of large and small houses in the area.

Social Change in the Area During the Last Century

The turn of the century brought in many improvements in local services. Milford had had gas lighting since 1884, but it was not until 1914 that gas streetlights arrived in Witley, and electricity services were installed in 1932. The water supply which had been piped earlier was still giving cause for concern when, in 1914, the vicar of Witley complained to the Parish Council that sometimes the water was milky white and at other times chocolate brown depending on the state of the pipes. Poor arrangements for sewage disposal had also been a continuing cause for complaint. A stream called the River Wit ran down Church Lane and past the school until it was piped underground sometime after 1918.

The road in Witley Street was first surfaced with tar in 1907, at a cost of £13.2s, funded by public subscription arranged by Mr. E. A. Chandler. The Smith Charities, set up through the bequest of Anthony Smith in 1669, were now run by the Parish Council who, in 1910, decided to award more realistic sums of money to fewer people meeting specific criteria. This fund now forms part of a charitable fund from which grants are still allocated each year to deserving local causes.

Archdeacon Potter, who owned Rake Manor (formerly our ancient Rake Mill) between 1907 and 1925, commissioned Baillie Scott to build the Women's Institute building in Milford. This was known locally as Potters Hall and is now the village hall, housing the parish council offices. The building was modelled on the billiards room at Rake.

In Witley, the community hall had been the 'Womens Hut', donated and re-erected in Church Lane by the Canadian Forces when they left Witley Camp. The hut is still used today by the Witley Brownies and Girl Guide groups. The parish was delighted when, in 1935, Mrs. Spencer Chichester of Enton Hall built a new village hall in memory of her late husband, Major Spencer Frederick Chichester. The hall stands at the north edge of the recreation ground with a verandah overlooking the cricket pitch and was described as the *finest hall of its size in the South of England*. Built by the local builders, Milton and Sons, from Witley, the hall boasted a powerful 'up-to-date electro-gramophone, with two amplifiers concealed over vent-ilators in the ceiling', installed by Mr. G. Wootton of Witley.

With the onset of the First World War, the vicar led a cavalcade of cars full of Witley men to Stoughton Barracks. 65 of them were not to return, that is nearly 3% of the local population. The surrounding villages also suffered their share of the losses. Chiddingfold lost 45 men, Grayswood 17 men, Milford and Thursley each lost 23 men.

Under special bye-laws, the Secretary of State for the War Department created, on 27th January 1915, a camp on Witley Common for training Canadian Soldiers before they went to France. The camp straddled the main road from London to Portsmouth and the road from Milford to

Haslemere, covering a plot of 1.5 miles long and 1.5 miles wide. Local tradesmen from Godalming constructed temporary buildings out of wood and corrugated iron to provide lock-up shops and services, and this became known as 'Tin Town'. The camp was occupied between early 1916 and September 1919, being used as a demobilization camp after the Armistice. Between 30,000 and 50,000 Canadian soldiers passed through the camp.

'Tin Town'. Produced courtesy of John Young.

In June 1940, 200 French boys between the ages of 14 and 16 years old were billeted at Rake, to be trained by General De Gaulle's état-major before becoming part of the elite military academy of Saint Cyr. This group, called 'L'école militaire des cadets de la France', occupied the barns of Rake Manor and the old Sattenham barns which were part of the Rake estate. The cadets were honoured, on 30th December 1940, by a visit from General De Gaulle himself. Escorted by the local home guard, he took the salute and donated £100 to be distributed to the cadets. Soon afterwards, on 4th February 1941, the cadets moved to a public school in Malvern, where the accommodation was more suitable.

Just two months later, a German Heinkel aircraft, one of nearly 300 on the way to a bombing raid of Birmingham, was shot down and crashed at Bramley. In the fight, bombs were jettisoned, but the plane clipped some trees when flying low over Busbridge Lakes and landed in a nearby field. Three crew were killed and are buried in Milford cemetery, one gunner survived.

The army huts on Rodborough Hill, which later became the home of Rodborough Hill School. Reproducesd courtesy of John Young.

After the War, in 1951, Rodborough Hill School was established in a series of huts on Rodborough Common near Moushill. The site had previously been the Algonquin Military Camp, occupied by the Canadian Army during World War Two. When the school was established, the Canadian commander of the camp, Brigadier A. Hamilton Gault, sent this message of goodwill to the staff and pupils of Rodborough Hill School:

'That yours may be a record of high purpose and loyalty to the traditions and ideals which unite the British Commonwealth and Empire under one Crown, and in the interests of peace, humanity and decency'.

Rodborough School moved to its present site in 1960. The Millennium year therefore marks the 50th anniversary of the school's opening and the school continues to be proud of its links with Canada.

In this book I have tried to include the main events which have shaped our community from the earliest time of mankind's influence.

A more detailed description of the way of life here during the last century is recounted in the vivid and often humorous recollections of local inhabitants to be found in 'Witley and Milford in Living Memory' by Valerie Box.

Although our heritage is not necessarily our future, if we understand our past we shall be better informed as we make decisions about our community for the future.

Further Reading

Chapter 1

Surrey Archaeological Collections Vol. 65, p130.
'British Regional Geology. The Wealden District.' 4th ed.
Surrey Archaeological Collections Vol. 64, p16-18.
'Climate History of the Modern World.' 2nd ed. H.H. Lamb.
Surrey Archaeological Collections Vol. 68, p198-201.
'Non–Belgic Iron Age in Surrey.'M. Bishop. Surrey Archaeological Collections Vol. 68.
'Placenames of Surrey.' Gover, Mawer and Stenton 1934.
'The Roman Villa at Whitebeech, Chiddingfold.' Gower and Gower 1984. Surrey Archaeological Collections Vol. 75.
'The 4th C Romano-British pottery kilns at Overwey, Tilford.' Surrey Archaeological Collections Vol. 51, p29-56.
'Romano-British cemeteries at Haslemere and Charterhouse.' Surrey Archaeological Collections Vol. 51, p1-28.
'Surrey' Domesday Book. Published by Phillimore.
Surrey Archaeological Collections Vol. 82, p1-168.
'Saxon Secrets in Surrey.' R. Poulton 1990.
'Saxon Surrey.' R. Poulton. In 'The Archaeology of Surrey to 1540.', 1987.
'Early Medieval Surrey.' J. Blair 1991.
'Dictionary of English Placenames.' Prof. Eckert 1959

Chapter 2

'The Domesday Book. England's Heritage Then and Now.' ed. Thomas Hinde 1985.
'Early Medieval Surrey.' J. Blair 1991
'Saxon Secrets in Surrey.' R. Poulton 1990
'Surrey.' Domesday Book. Published by Phillimore.
'Catteshall Mill.' A. and G. Crocker. Surrey Archaeological Society, Res. Vol. No. 8.
'The Watermills of Surrey.' Derek Stidder.
'Climate History of the Modern World.' H. H. Lamb.
'The Archaeology of Surrey to 1540.' ed. J. Bird and D. G. Bird 1987.
'Place Names of Surrey.' Gover, Mawer and Stinton.
Listed buildings, Witley Parish Council.
Victoria County History Vol. 3.
'On the Moated Site at Grayswood, Survey of the Manor of Witley, 1547–9.' C. Warner, with Greta Turner and Ella Bubb. Unpublished 1993.
'South Park Medieval Moated Homestead, Grayswood Nr. Haslemere.' Surrey Archaeological Society. Haslemere Educational Museum.
Woods Collection. Vols. 15 and 16. Godalming Museum.
'English Society in the Early Middle Ages.' D. M. Stenton.
'On an Fourteenth Century Rental of the Principal Manor of Godalming.' P. C. Woods. Surrey Archaeological Collections Vol. 23, p92.
'The Honour of Aquila.' E. A. Chandler 1911.'The Roman Villa at Whitebeech, Chiddingfold.' Gower and Gower 1984. Surrey Archaeological Collections Vol. 75.
'The Romanesque Wall Paintings of All Saints Church, Witley, Surrey.' David Park M.A. Courtauld Institute of Art 1981.

'Witley Lives.' W. Charles Palmer 1971. Private publication.
'Rake Manor, Godalming, Surrey.' A Bott. Surrey Archaeological Collections Vol. 80.
Surrey Archaeological Collections Vol. 23, p106.
'Pembroke Castle Birthplace of the Tudor Dynasty.' R. Innes – Smith.
'The Church of All Saints Witley.' Edward J. Newill 1916.
'Survey of the Manor of Witley 1547-49.' PRO LR2/190.

Chapter 3

Woods Collection. Vols. 15 and 16. Godalming Museum.
'Survey of the Manor of Witley.' 1547-1549
'Rake in Witley and the Ironworks on Witley and Thursley Heaths.' M. Guissepi 1903.
Witley Lives. C. Palmer 1971. Private publication.
'Bygone Haslemere.' Swanton and Woods.
'Peat cutting on Thursley Heath.' LM5/1/129 1657.
'Listed Buildings in Witley.' Witley Parish Council..
'Climate History of the Modern World.' H. H. Lamb.
'The Red Rose Leasehold'. E. A. Chandler 1911.
'The Watermills of Surrey.' D. Stidder.
'Catteshall Mill.' D. Crocker. Res. Vol. Surrey Archaeological Collections. No.8. 1981.
'Rake Manor, Godalming.' A. Bott. Surrey Archaeological Collections Vol. 80.
'British Regional Geology. The Wealden District.'
'The Iron Industry of the Weald.' H. Cleere and D. Crossley.
'Non-Belgic Iron Age in Surrey.' M. W. Bishop. Surrey Archaeological Collections Vol. 68.
'Roman Britain.' Peter Salway. Claredon Press. 1981.
Victoria County History. Vol. 2.
'Iron Ore Workings in the Western Weald.' B. C. Worssam. Prc. Geol. Asn. LXXV. 1964.
'Wealden Iron.' Straker 1931.
'The Place of Godalming in the Hosiery and Knitwear Industry; History and Products.'
Glenys Crocker. Surrey Archaeological Collection. Vol. 81.

Chapter 4

'A History of the Southern Railway.' C. F. Dendy Marshall.
'The Southern Railway, 1923-47.' R. A. Savill 1951.
'The South Western Railway.' C. H. Ellis 1956.
'Early Railways in Surrey.' C. E. Lee 1944.
'The London and South Western Railway. The formative years.' R. A. Wilkinson 1967.
'Thomas Brassey, Railway Builder.' Charles Walker 1969.
'The History of Railways in Britain.' F. Ferneyhough 1975.
'Surrey Industrial Archaeology.' G. A. Payne 1977.
Victoria County History. Vol. 2. 1911.
'Semaphore House Centenary.' J. K. Green 1947.
'Witley Lives.' W. C. Palmer, 1971. Private publication.
'The Buildings of England–Surrey.' I. Nairn and N. Pevsner 1962.
'Bygone Haslemere.' E. W. Swanton 1914.
'Helen Allingham's cottage homes –Revisited.' Annabel Watts.
'The Happy England of Helen Allingham.' Marcus B. Huish 1985.